It was hard to put down *Beyond Grief* since I started reading; it is really an amazing and very practical book. I thank Simret for sharing her darkest moment, her pain, and how she is overcoming it by God's sufficient grace. It helped me to gain more understanding about Heaven, and reading Pastor Leon's explanation about it really delivered my mind, and I thank God for that. So many things I learned and already started to apply to myself as I am grieving my mom's loss. I am encouraged to be more proactive to offer support to those who need it. *Beyond Grief* also made me think of how I spoke to people who are grieving in the past. It helped me to be more conscious and careful of what I say and how I act with people who are grieving. I really admire Simret's strength, courage, and resiliency to go through the difficult time she went through (maybe still going through) so gracefully. I believe her story will touch so many grieving hearts and give them hope to overcome.

Serkadis Atnafu Tadesse, Registered Nurse

I found *Beyond Grief* to be [an] informative and practical book for a grieving person and for anyone who is passing through challenges. Simret's courage gives you the insight on what to expect during dark moments of life. Simret's life shows us that it's both possible and reasonable to move forward by leaning on God's grace.

Dr. Michael Habteyonas

I am blessed to review *Beyond Grief*, a book with an insight for the process of grieving and the hope we can attain by leaning on God's grace. It is a practical book. I thank Simret for her vulnerability in sharing her most challenging moments, her horrific pain, and how she is overcoming it by God's sufficient grace. I am encouraged to be more proactive to offer support to those who are grieving a loss. I believe Simret's story will minister to so many grieving hearts and give them hope to overcome. I hope to see this book in your shelf.

Dr. Gebru Woldu / InternationalEvangelist Author of
*Gifts of the Holy Spirit & How to Use Them, and
The Dynamics of the Holy Spirit*

Beyond Grief is an inspirational, informative, and practical guide for those who are struggling with grief. Simret's personal journey empowers you to see God's amazing grace in the midst of grief while providing hope and healing for your hurting soul.

Jody Almond, Founder of
Solution Ministry and
Author of *Going All In*

Beyond Grief is practical, firsthand information centered on the day-to-day life of a family after a great loss. It is inspiring, takes the reader through different stages of grief and the triggers for each stage. It also provides some clinical insights from the perspectives of the bereaved that provides wider rays of light into the mind of the bereaved and the workability of each practical coping strategies. Definitely Faith and Hope for the future gained through practice of Spirituality by the bereaved provide a great anchor while navigating through the grief process. A great read for any individual and families going through grief and loss.

Georginia Nwoke, R. Psychologist AB.
Gilead Psychology Services, Calgary AB
Author *110 Nuggets for Excellent Parenting*

BEYOND GRIEF

A PERSONAL JOURNEY OF DEALING WITH GRIEF BY LEANING ON GOD'S AMAZING GRACE

SIMRET ARAYA GHEBREMARIAM

Foreword by Leon Fontaine
TV Host and Author of *The Spirit Contemporary Life and Supernatural Promises*

Printed in the United States of America

Published by Author Academy Elite

ISBNs:
Paperback: 978-1-64746-728-9
Hardback: 978-1-64746-729-6
Ebook: 978-1-64746-730-2

Available in hardcover, softcover, and e-book.

All Scripture quotations, unless otherwise
indicated, are taken from the Holy Bible,

Amplified Bible (AMP), Zondervan and
The Lockman Foundation, 2015.
Amplified Bible Classic Version (AMPC),
The Lockman Foundation, 1987.
Good News Translation (GNT), American Bible Society, 1976.
New International Version (NIV), Zondervan, 1978.
New King James Version (NKJV), James Nelson, 1982.
New Living Translation (NLT), Tyndale House Foundation, 2007.

For Aba Father,

Thank you for your divine protection, provision, and continuous supply. Thank you for the outworking of Your grace in my life.

You have given me everything that I need for life and goodliness. Therefore, I live and move and have my being in You, in Jesus' name. Amen.

In loving memory of Isaiah (Esayas) Tekle,

*Alganesh Ghebrezgabher and
Araya Ghebremariam*

*True saints who lived to lift
the spirit of the forlorn.*

*"Precious in the sight of the Lord is the
death of his saints." Psalm 116:15*

TABLE OF CONTENTS

Part 1: Dealing with the Pain of Grief

Part 2: Allowing the Pain to lessen

Part 3: Moving Forward

Part 4: Helping a Grieving Person

Part 5: God's Grace and Mercy

FOREWORD

Many people ask, why does God allow…?

Such a question might come out of someone's hurt or loss, which many pastors feel like their goal in life is to minimize people's pain and give several answers that don't align with what the Bible teaches. You have to be careful with that because minimizing someone's pain doesn't help them understand how to stop the pain, and it may leave a wrong picture about God in their belief system. I've met many men and women who don't want to go to church because their dad died when they were very young, and someone told them it was God's will or God wanted them in heaven. And others say God allowed the pain to teach us something. I found that many brilliant people say things like, "Well, the Bible will never be able to explain why bad things happen to good people." They say the Bible isn't clear, so we're never going to know. Perhaps one day, when we get to heaven, we'll be able to figure that out.

I say, with the principles that govern our lives, it's here—it's in the Bible now.

Others may believe if good comes out of bad, God allowed the wrong things to happen. This way of thinking is incorrect because it makes God look so small. God doesn't need to allow pain and catastrophe to teach us something; neither does He need a bad thing to make good things happen. We live in a fallen world, and bad things happen to good people because there's an enemy. Most people have a humanistic view of how life works. They have a different understanding of God and the issues in the world. They have a physical view of how life works, but they don't see the spirit realm, which happens to be behind it all. Many Christians don't study God's word and can be easily shaken when storms hit home. Believing in the Bible isn't enough; you should study and know the doctrines and understand its covenants. God is sovereign, which means all-powerful, but pastors change it to suggesting that God made a promise, and He might allow this or that in your life. However, when someone loses a baby or dies in a car incident, how do you explain it? Most believers have developed a way of thinking that it's just God who's responsible for allowing the devastation. However, when you think that way, it creates an enormous amount of problems in Christ's body as it puts the responsibility on God for all the damages that the enemy caused. I have observed such teachings severed a relationship of innocent people with their loving Creator.

The Bible teaches there are spiritual dynamics and a spirit realm that keeps trying to influence the physical realm. The Bible doesn't say things happen naturally. In fact, it says there's an enemy behind it all. God isn't focusing on every individual and telling the devil to stop after a certain point. "No temptation has overtaken you except what is common to mankind. And God is faithful; he will not let you be tempted beyond what you can bear. But when you are tempted, he will also provide a way out so that you can endure it" (1

Corinthians 10:13 [New International Version]). Sadly, the verse gets interpreted to say God will let us be tempted. But if you are a new testament believer, you are a new creation. You're equipped to take anything thrown at you, not that God allows a specific amount of temptation before he stops the enemy. When the devil tempted Jesus, it showed Satan was the god of this world.

When Jesus died on the cross, he dissolved Satan's ability to get in you. If you believe God's word and recognize the spiritual realm, you can cooperate with God to manifest his will and blessing. John 10:10 (NIV) says, Satan comes to steal, kill, and destroy, but Jesus came so we may have life and have it more abundantly. Not having a working knowledge of the spirit doesn't set you free, and it also worsens any predicament you are trying to overcome. Once you know the spirit realm, you begin to understand things truly in your heart. As He shows you this, and the Holy Spirit is guarding you, Satan becomes afraid of you.

There's no simple answer to why untimely death happens, even though people want to believe there's a simple answer to everything. For example, if I ask a doctor where did this cancer come from, he would have to think back through all the years of study, and he may come back with different explanations about diet, chemicals, and genes. There's so much to go through, and if the doctor doesn't have enough background, it would take hours or days for him to answer that question. Humanists don't acknowledge God as a whole; they're either agnostic or atheist. Many Christians don't realize they're the same way if they don't study the word and keep giving explanations that don't help a hurting person.

In Colossians 1:27 (NIV), the Bible teaches about the mystery of the gospel hidden for generations and is now revealed or made known. I find so many people haven't dived into this precious word of God and found some of the mysteries that go with the new covenant—they're clueless. They superimpose the old testament teachings on the new testament while praying old testament prayers, using old testament principles. Now, the old testament principles will work if you take them through the cross. This is crucial because the new testament is a rewrite of the old testament. So, I want to challenge you to get into God's word because it has the answers to your questions.

Beyond Grief will help you discover the grace of God, which is the power of God that helps overcome any issues that come from the enemy. The enemy could hurt us; however, God is with us to empower us and help us go through any storm and prevail. "Finally, be strong in the Lord and his mighty power. Put on the full armor of God so that you can take your stand against the devil's schemes. For our struggle is not against flesh and blood, but against the rulers, against the authorities, against the powers of this dark world and against the spiritual forces of evil in the heavenly realms" (Ephesians 6:10-12, NIV).

I'm grateful for helping Simret to get hope and comfort in the word of God. I believe her journey and determination will inspire you. I know you will get some practical help to navigate your grieving journey or support others who are hurting using this book's tools.

Pastor Leon Fontaine
TV Host and Author of
The Spirit Contemporary Life and
Supernatural Promises

INTRODUCTION

It was Monday, March 22, 1999. I was sitting at the bedside of my mom, who was terminally ill. My sister, who came from Sweden, was sitting across the bed on a sofa with a couple of visitors. The room was quiet and very peaceful. My mom grabbed my hand and squeezed it as hard as she could. I asked her, "Do you need anything?" I thought she needed me to get her something. But, instead of answering my question, she made a sharp sound and rolled her eyes. I didn't know what to do, but my sister, who is a registered nurse, quickly checked my mom's pulse, covered her eyelids, shouted in anguish, "She is gone," and left the room, crying like crazy.

I was frozen, still holding my mom's hand, which slowly turned cold. The doctors told us she wouldn't make it; however, I didn't know she would be gone that soon. I wished she could've lived a bit longer, at least to see the wedding of my oldest brother that we were planning for the next year. I was sad and solemn, staring at my mom's beautiful face, and few women came into the room while the entire neighbourhood was wailing in our yard. Then, Adey Fana (our neighbor and best friend of my mom) came and took Mom's hand away from me and asked me to get out of the room as they needed to prepare the body. I said, "That's fine. I can help you." She thought I'd lost my mind because I didn't cry or show any reaction, but after realizing I meant it, she asked me to bring my mom's white clothes that she wore when taking holy communion. I went to Mom's closet, brought the beautiful outfit, and then helped them get warm water to soak the herbs they needed to wash and embalm the body. My mom looked very beautiful in her white clothes. I gave the body another glance, left the room quietly, found a dark hiding place in our storage room, sat down on the floor, and shed some tears. I was still shocked, but my heart was at peace.

We put my mom's body to rest near my dad's grave at St. Michael's cemetery in a village called Maedo, Eritrea. Both my parents were known for their humility, generosity, and wisdom. Our neighbours were devastated by my mom's departure. People mourned my mom for weeks. After several weeks, my two older sisters, who came from Canada and Sweden, left for their home. My two older brothers had gone back to the army, so I was the oldest in the house left to run the family business and look after my younger brother and youngest sister. Since the employees were very loyal to my parents, it wasn't hard to manage the family business. I also had lots of support from our relatives and neighbours, who adored my mom. However, my mom was my best friend, and I was sad for a very long time.

After about a year, I received a fully paid scholarship from the University of Life Science in Norway for my master's degree. I still had some time before I made my decision. I was unsure if I should leave; I would be leaving my youngest sister and brother behind. We had an Ethiopian nanny, who would be taking care of them for a while, but wouldn't that be tough for her? *What if our nanny left for her home? Did I need to search for an Eritrean nanny?* But we loved her, and she was part of our family. *Should I decline the scholarship? But if I went to Norway, I could get my studying done and find a well-paying job when I returned.* I thought to myself, *This is a once in a lifetime opportunity, and I should take it before it's too late.* So, I shared my decision with my siblings and our nanny and started preparing for the trip. Since then, my life went through various unpredictable journeys.

I studied in Norway for two years, and when I was preparing to return home, I received an alarming call from my friend who had just arrived in Sweden. After we chatted for a bit, I said, "Hey, Mary, I just wanted to tell you that I'm going home soon." There was silence for a few seconds, and then I heard her say, "Don't go back." I stood there frozen and very confused as to why I shouldn't go back. Shouldn't I see my family? "Wait, why shouldn't I?" I asked her. "The government closed our churches, and they started arresting our pastors. They aren't getting out anytime soon; it's too risky. Just go somewhere else and be safe." She hung up; I put the phone back in its slot and sat down thinking about where I could go. I sat at a bench, crying nonstop because I thought I might never see my family again. Immediately, I started looking for jobs in the entire world—except Eritrea. I made phone calls to everyone I knew in Europe, Australia, South Africa, Asia, and the USA.

I finally found a job at a farm in Leeds, England. My friend in London connected me to the farm owners in Leeds who agreed to hire me as their financial director. I was desperate, so I took it even though it wasn't my study field. The employer arranged all the paperwork, and I went from Ås, Norway, to Leeds, England.

I wasn't too fond of Leeds; perhaps I wasn't ready for the detour in my life. I became very depressed. To make matters worse, the people I met were rude and unkind. My boss was very stingy, and the job wasn't pleasant either. The skies were so cloudy, and it rained almost every day. After seven weeks in England, I couldn't stand it anymore. I always had to work extra hours for pay that was worse than decent, and the house I lived in wasn't worth the money I paid for it.

My dearest cousin, Kidane (I call him Kidun), lived in Canada. I decided to call him and ask if I could visit him in Canada; I wanted an escape. I'd never met him, but I heard lots of good things about him, and I used to write my aunt (his mom) a letter for him as she didn't know how to write or read. My sister gave me his phone number, and I started talking to him. He was amiable and open-minded. It didn't take us long to become friends—I was eager to see him.

One day, I called him. "Hello Simret?" my cousin said as he picked up.

"Hey Kidun, how are you?" I replied.

"I'm doing just fine! Is there anything going on?" he said with joy.

"I called you because I don't like England, and as you know, I can't go back to Eritrea. Do you think I could come and visit Ottawa for a little while?" I asked.

"Sure, you can stay here as long as you like. Let me know what you need?"

I got so excited I could finally leave England, although I had heard Canada was quite cold. He sent me an invitation to visit him; I got my ticket as soon as I got my visa, quit my job, and hopped on the plane to Ottawa.

While on the plane, I couldn't sleep, so I read facts about Canada in my book I bought at the airport. I didn't know Canada was the country with the best quality of life in the world. *Maybe I should consider staying until the government gets their heads straight in Eritrea*, I thought. I saw my sister, my cousin Kidun, his kids, and my other cousins waving at me at the airport. I took my luggage and headed towards them. I felt a huge relief being there with my family. I stayed at my sister's house for a month, and then I decided to find a job and stay in Canada.

After a couple of years, I got married and moved to Calgary. Recently, my husband Isaiah's tragic death left me with several unanswered questions, as he had big dreams in life, and I never thought we would lose him so soon. I have gone through many hardships in my life, and I'm not new to grieving. However, dealing with my recent grief was very complex; it felt like a very thick and dark cloud that no light could penetrate surrounded me. I had to choose whether to stand up to the challenge and overcome or do nothing and get defeated. I chose the former.

Throughout this book, I share my personal story of pain and how God's grace enabled me to prevail against the odds. Understandably, a few weeks after the tragedy, everyone seemed to move on, back to their everyday lives, but my family life would never be the same. This book takes you on my grieving journey from shock, denial, anger, guilt, pain, depression, and bitterness to forgiveness, self-care, acceptance, and gratitude.

Grieving cannot be done in a set time or put in a box and set away. Different people have different paces of healing. However, when we lean on God's grace, He is faithfully there with us amid our deepest sorrow. Only God can console our hearts and lead us forward with peace one step at a time.

Sometimes, our life seems unpredictable, but every day of our lives is an open book to our God who knew us before the very beginning of our lives. People think I'm strong, but that's far from the truth. I'm not strong; I've simply learned to lean on God's grace. In my weakness, He was and remains the source of my strength. He is always in me and with me to help me get through anything. "'Not by might nor by power but by my Spirit,' says the Lord Almighty" (Zechariah 4:6, NIV).

If you are grieving any loss, I hope this book will give you some tools for comfort and healing. I've also added some tips to encourage those supporting a grieving person to learn how not to add sorrow to the hurting person and instead become a competent supporter. Above all, we can all take advantage of God's grace to accelerate the healing process.

PART 1
DEALING
WITH THE PAIN
OF GRIEF

When I think of death, and of late the idea has come with alarming frequency, I seem at peace with the idea that a day will dawn when I will no longer be among those living in this valley of strange humors. I can accept the idea of my own demise, but I am unable to accept the death of anyone else.

I find it impossible to let a friend or relative go into that country of no return.

Disbelief becomes my close companion, and anger follows in its wake. I answer the heroic question "Death, where is thy sting?" with "it is here in my heart and mind and memories."

—Maya Angelou, "When I Think of Death"

1
YES, IT HURTS DEEPLY

I'm not too crazy about celebrating a New Year. By now, I know it's not the New Year that makes the difference; it's the goals I set, the plans I make, and the execution of those plans that make the difference. For the last few years, I've been doing my planning twice a year. January and July are usually my focus months. I review the gains and pains of the previous five months, set a few high-level goals I would like to achieve in the coming months, and prepare accordingly.

I was married to my late husband, Isaiah, in 2005 and had three kids together. Our life looked normal to the outsiders. However, we had been facing giants behind the closed door as my late husband struggled with an occasional but very dangerous drug addiction. After several failed attempts to help him, we finally decided to separate based on the advice from our professional counselors as his behavior was getting

3

worse, and it might have endangered our kids' lives. However, we had put a plan to continue our support for each other, and we communicated almost daily. Since he moved out, he seemed to put every effort into staying sober and getting his life together. He used to come home on the weekends to help me cook and clean the house. We used to go to church together, so only a few people knew we weren't living together.

I had a great start in 2018. Despite the difficulties in my life, I managed to finalize my OPUS (Overarching vision, Purpose, Unifying strategies, and Scorecard for significance) as part of my coaching certification with the Igniting Souls program. OPUS is an idea created by Chet Scott, who also wrote a book called *Becoming Built to Lead*. I used to write my short term and long-term goals before, but the OPUS framework helped me to go deeper and set the overall roadmap for my life. It helped me to analyze my life and prepare for the next level. I was ready to launch my coaching business and started enrolling clients into my program.

On January 20, 2018, Isaiah came to the house with his relative, who was new to Canada. They cleaned the house, then spent some time with the kids while I went to a spa to get my hair and nails done. After I came home, we ate supper, and they left around 8:00 p.m. Soon after, the kids and I did our evening routine and went to bed. Around 1:00 a.m., the house phone rang. I thought it was my brother from Eritrea calling to check on me, so I decided I would call him the next day and ignored it. But it didn't stop. So, I went to pick it up, half-asleep; it wasn't my brother. It was the relative who came with Isaiah. With desperation, he asked me if I could pick him up. He and Isaiah had argued, and he said he needed urgent help. I called close friends from church to join me and went there, but when I arrived, our friends from church were already there, so I allowed them to sort things out for the night, as I needed to be home.

The following day, I called Isaiah to check what happened. He said he would handle it himself and assured me everything would be fine. Again, I called him on my way to church around 4:00 p.m. and encouraged him to join us at the church, but he said he needed to rest. So, I contacted a couple of friends to follow up with him. While driving on the Deerfoot Highway, a new song came to my heart in my native language, and I started singing. "ትማሊ. ዘሕለፍካኒ: ንሎሚ እምነት ኮይኑኒ: ጽባሕወን ንስኻ ኣሎኻኒ: የለን ንዓይ ዘስግእኒ." The message speaks to having confidence in God for whatever comes our way. The translation is, "God, I trust You. What You have done for me so far has strengthened my faith and gives me courage to face any challenge that may come my way." I sang it several times.

On Monday, January 22, 2018, my 5:00 a.m. alarm went off. I forced myself out of bed to read that day's "Rhapsody of Realities" devotion shared by Pastor Chris Oyakhilome. I took a shower, got breakfast ready, and packed lunch for the kids before waking the kids and completing our morning routines. I felt a bit exhausted from the late night and anxious for Isaiah, sensing something wasn't right with him following the incident with his relative. I tried calling him, but he didn't answer. I tried my best not to think about it and dragged my focus back to the tasks at hand. I dropped my youngest and middle children at daycare and school. Then, I reminded my oldest not to play on electronics and to catch the school bus on time. Finally, I called my pastor to join me in checking on Isaiah.

At 7:10 a.m., we arrived at Isaiah's apartment. We continuously rang the bell without an answer. We tried his phone; it rang, but there was no response. We thought he was ignoring us since he usually turned off his phone when he was angry, but this time, it was ringing. We felt the need to get inside and check on him. The building maintenance office advised it was not legal to violate someone's privacy without their consent, but one of the ladies working there assured us she saw him the day prior, and he was fine.

"I am his wife," I said. "I can take responsibility. I just want to make sure he is ok."

Despite continued efforts to convince them, they held fast—I needed to call the police; only then could they open the door in the presence of a police officer.

By then, it was 8:30 a.m., and I needed to go to my company's annual kick-off meeting. I didn't feel like leaving, but the superintendent convinced me Isaiah was just fine. We finished our meetings around 4:30 p.m., and a couple of my friends asked me to stay, mingle over a cocktail, and chat. I explained I couldn't and ran back to Isaiah's apartment. I asked his neighbors if they could help me while repeatedly knocking at his door and ringing the bell for a long time—there was still no answer. I called the police and waited.

I waited for about an hour but eventually left my friends to wait for the police while I dashed to daycare, already late. Apologizing to the caregiver, I picked up my youngest daughter and collected my oldest from after-school care. At home, we changed our clothes to prepare our supper together. While the food cooked, the kids did their homework. Then, we ate supper.

As part of our evening routine, we read the "Rhapsody of Realities" devotional together. During tuck in, my middle child, Faith, said she couldn't sleep and wanted to wrap herself in Isaiah's bathrobe to read a book. I agreed, kissed her good night, and went to bed. I wanted to follow up with our friends about Isaiah's status, but I was physically and mentally exhausted—and scared to make the call. I fell into bed, and it wasn't long before I was fast asleep. Around 10:00 p.m., Faith came to my bed to tell me someone was knocking at our door. Rushing to the window half-asleep, I saw our pastor's car and the police car. My heart melted. I knew something was wrong but assumed maybe they found Isaiah unconscious and took him to the hospital. I didn't want to think about death, so I calmly opened the door and asked them if he was ok. The police officer and our pastor asked me to sit down, then shared the horrible news: they had found Isaiah's body inside his apartment. I thought I was dreaming. I couldn't believe it; I was numb.

"I have been fighting all these years, so this won't happen. It's not fair. This can't happen! I need to see him immediately," I cried.

They advised he was at a medical facility where they could do an autopsy; I wouldn't have access to him until I moved him to a funeral home.

"I saw him last night, and he was completely normal." I begged them, "Please, I need to see him." I felt if only I could see him, I could wake him.

They provided the facility's phone number, which I could call in the morning. After making sure I had emotional support, the policeman left. I was at a loss—what to say, what to think—and began crying. I felt confident he would wake up for me. I knew he hadn't completed his mission on earth—Isaiah had had three specific goals, none of which he accomplished.

I said to myself, *We possess the power to raise the dead, heal the sick, and cast out devils in the name of Jesus.* I started to meditate on the following verses and decided to keep meditating on them until I saw Isaiah. I thought God would simply raise him as His word said, "Heal the sick, cleanse the lepers, raise the dead, cast out devils" (Matthew 10:8, NKJV).

"But if the Spirit of him that raised up Jesus from the dead dwell in you, he that raised up Christ from the dead shall also quicken your mortal bodies by his Spirit that dwelleth in you" (Romans 8:11, NKJV).

Early the next morning, I contacted the medical facility to arrange to see him. They told me they couldn't allow me to see him there, only at the funeral home. With help from our beloved senior pastor and friend, Meron, we found the funeral home and arranged the transfer of Isaiah's body. I immediately called the funeral home and spoke with the manager. I implored them to expedite the transfer and viewing as soon as it was possible. The woman on the phone asked me if I was sure I wanted to see him before they prepared him. I didn't care; I felt an overwhelming desire to see him immediately. The next morning, my friends gathered at my home, and I asked them to pray for God to wake him as Jesus did with Lazarus.

Finally, Wednesday morning, the funeral home allowed me to see him. The pastors of our church were genuinely supporting me and praying with me for God to raise him. We continued to pray during the entire drive there. When we entered, we told the funeral home staff we were there to pray. They graciously allowed us. We prayed, we shouted, we did whatever we could. No change. I slept on the funeral home floor, pleading with God. It was then I saw a vision—a warm blanket surrounding me, and my heart was filled with song. I knew God was with me through everything I would need to face.

Grasping onto that vision, I asked my pastors to take me home so I could start arranging the funeral.

I started groaning and crying. "He didn't wake up! I thought he would. This isn't fair!" (I'm still weeping as I'm writing this.)

By God's grace, I managed to recall Isaiah's wishes when he'd considered how he'd like his funeral to be and began to write everything down. Requesting my dearest, beloved friend, Deborah, to carry out his wishes, I provided the details, and she and a team organized everything perfectly to the last detail. I had little experience with funerals in Canada, having attended only one funeral for a church brother, who passed a year before Isaiah. Isaiah had organized that specific funeral, taking pride in every detail, sharing highlights with me, and even assigning me a couple of tasks. Actively involved in the social affairs of the people at our church and our local community, Isaiah was on the front line to support anyone needing help. Who knew I would be using the information he shared with me to arrange his funeral? *Sigh*!

Monday, January 28, 2018, was the day of the funeral. I struggled with mixed feelings. While in denial of what was happening around me and still in shock, the presence of God was so obvious, almost tangible, that my heart was full of an indescribable peace. The community of people praying for me lifted me.

We arrived minutes before the service started to a packed church. Isaiah knew a lot of people. He was a beloved friend to many, and he loved helping and being there for our community, who was shocked by the news. As is the Ethio-Eritrean tradition, women wept and chanted aloud, but I focused on supporting my kids, who wished to see him and say goodbye. I gathered my kids to the casket and said our final goodbye, still feeling the warmth of God's presence.

Honoring God in everything, as the program started, I got up and lifted my hands, worshipping God with the choir. On a beautiful, sunny day, we interred the body in its resting place. Just a body now, Isaiah wasn't here; he was in Heaven rejoicing with his Aba Father. To my surprise, I felt calm, as though I was watching a movie. The crowd was wailing, and the sound from the traditional chanting was deafening, but I still couldn't process anything.

A few weeks passed, and one by one, I witnessed people return to normal life. I knew our lives would never go back to what it was. Struggling to know where to start, I wanted to run from life. To some extent, I was jealous—Isaiah didn't have to deal with life's day-to-day challenges anymore, let alone answer the tough questions the kids were asking. Not wanting to wake up but needing to serve and comfort my kids, I sucked it up. Pretending to be ok, I'd get up and cook breakfast, send the kids to school, and drop my youngest at the day home. Privately, I would get into my closet to weep and write poems releasing my feelings. One of the many poems was titled "He Made the Graveyard Rich."

A precious soul, a precious gem
Full of beauty, full of dream
Full of energy, full of passion
Without notice, he went too soon
There was a lot to be done
A restaurant to open
A book to be written
Children to have risen
There was a ministry burning in his heart
Serving all was his prime mandate
His running feet are still
His thunder voice is no more here
His swift eyes are closed
His giving hands are clamped
He was dying inside
While smiling outside
And no one understood...
He knew how to comfort
He knew how to reach out
He knew when to chat
He knew when to be silent
Full of wisdom full of talents
He was equipped with lots and lots...
We haven't withdrawn
All that can be given
He died so rich, Isaiah went too soon
but his loving memory will remain!

My tears flowed with my feelings onto the paper. (I wept again later when I read through my notes.) I only emerged from my closet when my kids came home. I would cook and try to eat with them, though I had no appetite. At times, I would excuse myself, instructing my oldest to look after his sisters, so I could lock myself in my room to cry more. Then, I'd wash my face to pretend I was ok again.

A couple of weeks into my mourning period, I thought work would distract me. God bless my director. He would call me every morning from Winnipeg to check on me. Some days, I couldn't hold it in, weeping endlessly into the phone. He never hung up, though, and showed his continued support. He genuinely did whatever he could to support me, but I was obviously not ready to be at work. Since I worked from home, most days were filled with me crying on my desk while I pushed myself to add value.

After three days back to work, one of my colleagues texted me to join her for lunch at a nearby restaurant. Over lunch, she shared her story of loss. She imparted lots of tips for self-care and encouraging me not to force myself. She suggested for me to take the time I needed to process everything slowly. (I am forever thankful for this, Monique Ferguson.)

It hurts to deal with the aftermath. At first, I got loads of support from everyone, but after the first month, everyone returned to their day-to-day demands of life. The decision to take a leave of absence from work was difficult since I'm a workaholic who can't sit down and do nothing. Of course, there was a lot to be done at home—from cooking to cleaning—but housework isn't my strength. I like writing, coordinating, challenging, managing, moving things to the next level, but at that time, I was in a dead zone without motivation for anything. My source of energy at that moment was my youngest sister, Semhar, my friends who support me through social media, and the "Rhapsody of Realities" daily devotional message from my mentor, Pastor Chris. I don't think Pastor Chris knows me, but I call him my mentor because his books and teachings have served me for the past ten years, and I have read "Rhapsody of Realities" for the past five years daily. Despite feeling a lack of connection to God at that time, I continued to do the confession and reading of the daily devotional book.

A few weeks following the incident, a wave of sudden, outrageous emotion started to boil inside me. I was angry at everyone, including myself. I was furious with Isaiah for the choices he made. I was frustrated with myself for feeling like I didn't do enough to prevent it. I was even upset with the church, feeling they hadn't done enough for Isaiah despite his commitment to serve them. I was boiling inside. All I wanted to do was scream, but with my little one with me most of the time, I had to wait until her nap time. I'd retreat back into my closet to sob, covering myself with pillows, screaming as loud as I could. It was a horrible season.

Different people had different opinions about the tragedy; while well-meaning, some of the things they did and said hurt more than helped. It hurt when friends complained their husbands didn't do their chores while knowing I'd never see mine again. It hurt when the people I thought would be there to support me disappeared one by one. It hurt to feel like God failed me. And it hurt to accept my children were fatherless unnecessarily. It was so painful and such a profound hurt.

2
DEALING WITH REGRETS

Isaiah lived to give; he served anyone he could with joy regardless of whether they were rich or poor, male or female, young or old. He served in so many ways: shoveling snow, mowing grass, cleaning their house, cooking, translating, taking people to the hospital, arranging funerals, picking up at the airport, sponsoring refugees, doing paperwork for start-up business owners, praying, sharing the gospel, and uplifting others. His phone rang day and night, but he never minded. My son and I used to call him 911, as he would make himself available anytime for anyone in need to talk or get his support. I received several testimonies of his kindness from people that I knew and from strangers. A few months after his passing, I noticed the following message on Isaiah's obituary site:

When Isaiah and I met, we were both on separate paths of healing. The friendship and experience of meeting Isaiah for me are more than words can ever fully convey to whoever reads this. We came from different backgrounds, different generations, and different worlds. When we came into each other's lives, I was self-destructive and filled with hate; I came from a place where hope is rare and evil thrives. As soon as I met him, he showed me a light that I remembered seeing somewhere some time in my past. He asked if I would pray with him, and so I sat beside him, and we prayed. We spent time with one another and got to know each other. He shared his struggles and pain with me and me with him. He came to call me his brother and he mine. The time we spent together was more helpful to me than anything; he showed me light when things were dark, he gave me strength when I was broken, he gave me faith when I had none. He shared his thoughts and culture with me, took me in, and gave me a golden paged Bible as a token of our friendship. After our time together, he would message me to ask how I'm doing and let me know he prays and thinks of me; I'm ashamed to say I fell back into the dark and went back to my old ways. But what happened the summer that followed changed me forever. So I got into some trouble with the law and was trying to make my way down south to Medicine Hat from Red Deer. I had [a] sawed-off .22 in my waist and a stolen Honda Civic. I made it to the Deerfoot Calgary, and the car broke down. So now, I'm high on drugs walking away from a stolen vehicle on the side of the Deerfoot with a gun in my waist. I make it to the next exit and get into a residential area. I'm hungry and lost have no direction or clue what is going to happen with me or care for that matter. I hate myself and barley have the strength to keep on living. I remember thinking death would be easy; no one would care or miss me, but I keep on walking. Eventually, I made it to a convenience store in a small strip mall, my phone was dead, so I planned on stealing a charger. Except when I went inside, I decided to start talking to the person working behind the counter and ask if they would be so kind as to charge my phone for me. I was outside the Max waiting for my phone to get a charge, on the curb, thinking about how I'm going to get down south. When out of nowhere, I heard my name, I look over and at one off the lowest points and most depressing times of my life when I don't think anything is going to be ok. Who else but my brother, Isaiah, pulled up and took me for a talk. When he saw me, he didn't like what he saw. I was skinny and not healthy, but that didn't matter to him. He took me out for food, and talked with me, and was there for me as my brother with no judgment whatsoever. I thought to myself, what are the chances of him spotting me sitting there in a city with over 1,000,000 people in that neighborhood that the vehicle broke down by, at a point where I may not have had the strength to lived out the day. In my mind, the odds were astronomical because it wasn't chance I met him, it wasn't chance he saved me that day, it wasn't random that we became brothers, it was the Lord working in his mysterious way. We talked for an hour, and I brushed the meeting off for whatever reason and ended up making it to where I was going. A few weeks later, I got into a high-speed chase with the RCMP and was arrested with multiple felonies. I eventually was convicted and spent my time in prison for my sins. The whole time I was in jail, Isaiah kept popping into my head. His words of wisdom and hope, his strength and courage, he told me I deserve a chance to be happy and that I'm loved by God and worth more than the darkness that I was surrounded by. His words and presence that day was a blessing given to me. I listened to my brother and got away from everything I've ever known because I believed him and didn't believe that he just happened to find me that day God meant for him to save me in my time of need. Even though I couldn't save my brother, I will for the rest of my days on this earth live my life to share what he shared with me a chance to live, a chance to hope, a chance to love. I will open

my heart and spread his message of the Lord in the hope that
I can save a lost soul like he saved mine. I love you, brother,
and will think of you often, tears today, but blessed to know
you will be there when my journey ends. I will pray for your
family to have strength during this time of loss, and lastly,
thank you again, my friend.

(This message puts tears in my eyes every time I read it.)
I remember Isaiah telling me about the divine coincidence
and us praying for this person together. Isaiah was a selfless
servant leader. The message above is one of the many stories
people would share of his love and service.

My first regret, I wish I had encouraged him to serve more
people. Honestly, I was not happy with his overcommitting
himself to helping others, and I always argued he should give
his health priority and stand steady first. At times, I also got
annoyed when I witnessed some people taking advantage of
him. Now, it seems like his life was meant to be short, and
he needed to serve.

Isaiah had also served his family and siblings generously.
For example, he would set aside time to ensure he talked to
all of his siblings regularly, depending on their availability.
He was a great listener and wise advisor, so he wouldn't mind
if anyone dumped their problems on him. He would take it
seriously, fast, and pray about any issue he discussed with
anyone and provide advice when necessary. He would cook
and clean for our family and make sure he sat down for dinner
with the kids. He would invite people he knew were struggling
or new to Canada, feed their stomachs from his delicacy, and
encourage them through the word of God regardless of their
religion. Most people said they were always fed both physically
and spiritually when they were with Isaiah. Another friend
explained: "When Isaiah steps into any crowd, the light bulb
turns on." He was indeed a shining light! Me, I was the balance.
I help others when I can, but I am a firm believer in assisting

myself before I can help others. "Love others as much as you love yourself" (Matthew 22:39 [GNT]). I love people, but I couldn't function at his level of energy.

My second regret is while he was too busy helping people and I was too busy on personal growth, I didn't spend quality time with him. Isaiah wasn't working for most of the years we lived together; I was committed to providing a good lifestyle for my family. I was often future-focused, busy either taking courses or working on my next project. He always complained about my busy schedule, and I complained about his busy schedule serving others. Despite his lifestyle, at least he cooked and ate with the kids every time he was home, while I barely sat down with them. He used to say one day I would regret it. Yes, I do regret it now.

My third and biggest regret, I should have done something to prevent his death. Several questions bombarded my mind—why didn't I ask them to sleepover Saturday night? What if I'd broken into his apartment Monday morning? Why hadn't I asked him for a spare key? Hopeless wishes and questions were eating me up alive.

Naturally, I am a problem solver. When I realized death was something I couldn't solve, I felt so defeated. People tried to comfort me by saying things like, "You have done everything you can; we are proud of you." Still, deep inside of me, I'm not convinced I had done enough. Yes, I fought a lot, tried a lot, searched for a solution a lot, but what's the point? I didn't achieve my plan to sustain his life. I felt all my hard work was in vain. Death wouldn't give me any more chances to find the solution and take action. It's done and gone, and I felt helpless. I thought I was such a loser!

I had access to wise mentors and wrote them emails stating all my regrets and asked for advice. Their answer was short but to the point. "...*if you think you didn't do enough to help rescue your husband, ask God to forgive you and forget it because our God is merciful. Note: Your husband is gone. There is nothing you can do for him now. But you can do something about your future and final home. God bless you."*

At first, I thought their answer was a bit harsh, but when I meditated on it several times, I knew it was the hard truth I needed to swallow. So, I have decided to take the time to stay at the throne of Aba's mercy and grace. I tried to confront death, tried to solve death, and my emotions went all over the place, but I knew I needed to reach a place of acceptance. I asked and received forgiveness by faith for all the reasons I felt guilty and have decided to learn from my experience and lean on God's grace for the rest of my life.

3
BLAMING GOD WON'T REDUCE OUR PAIN

I had a personal encounter with God by believing in Jesus Christ as my savior about twenty-four years ago. Since then, I have never doubted God loves me, and His presence is within me. Ever since that time, I have this overwhelming peace inside me that I can't describe in words. Through several challenges, including my parents' death in my early twenties, God's peace was always with me, and I have never blamed God. After the tragedy of my husband's death, I honestly thought God would raise him because I was so sure Isaiah hadn't fulfilled his purpose. I believed and prayed for God to raise him, but it didn't go the way I expected.

I waited a few weeks till everyone went home and set aside seven days to mourn my husband and seven days to argue with God. During my solitary mourning, I wrote several poems, which I may publish some other time. For now, I want to share my argument with God. My only question was: "God, I know You are omnipotent. I have seen You rescuing Isaiah from several deaths before. Why did he die now?" Isaiah wasn't overly ambitious, but he had three specific goals in his life: to preach the gospel, to write books, and to open a restaurant. He always spoke about those three goals. He was living the first goal and had a unique way of ministering to people; I never saw anyone reject Christ after he talked to them. In 2017 alone, he led three families, including the grandparents, to Christ, coached five youths, and taught AWANA Bible class to children every Wednesday. He openly spoke about his weaknesses, and yet he was a magnet to people. He loved writing; the kids and I treasure the twelve notebooks he left filled with his handwriting. Hopefully, one day either our children or I will publish some books from them. Isaiah was a great communicator, an excellent cook, and I know his passion for food and people would have made him a successful restaurant owner. So why God?

I received no answer. I asked the same question for the entire week but didn't hear anything back. Then, slowly, I started to lose my confidence in God. I hated life, and intense rage at God began to build in me. I felt life was meaningless and not worth living. During that period, I remember one day an elderly lady, whom Isaiah brought to Christ, called me and asked me for prayer. I said, "Okay, Mom, I will pray for you later." I didn't want to offend her, but I knew I wouldn't pray; my faith was gone. I didn't want to wake up from bed; everything was dark. While I was in that dark season, a few women came to visit me from church one day, and they started singing. I didn't have any appetite for singing at all. Then my dear friend Richo held my hands and said in Amharic, "No worries, Simri, just sing even if you don't feel like it." In my heart, I said, *Even the Bible told us to let the one who is happy sing, can't you see I am sad and miserable?* But I didn't say anything to her and just kept weeping. Then they prayed for me and left.

The next morning, an old friend from the University of Asmara, who lives in Kurdistan, sent me a message titled "Born for Love" on my Facebook messenger. The note said, *"We are loved. Born out of love, into love, to know love, and to be loved. Yes, we were born into a fallen, sorry world, which is, at the same time, more lovely than any fairy tale. It is both. And in this beautiful, heartbreaking world, God—the eternal, omniscient, amazing One—loves human beings. Including you. Especially you."* My immediate thought was, *Really? If he loved me, why did he make me a widow at such a young age?* It helped me to raise another argument with God: "Do You even love me?" Then after a couple of days again, she sent me: *"God is within her; she will not fall; God will help her at the break of day"* (Psalm 46:5, NIV). Since then, my friend Tsigereda Haile kept sending me different encouraging and thought-provoking messages that would help me reconsider my argument with God.

Another old friend from Norway started calling to check on me. I'm usually a transparent person; I told her I was angry at God. I was in deep sadness and couldn't even sleep. She listened and prayed a short prayer for me and started to call me every evening before I went to sleep. Sometimes, she shared the word of God and prayed for me. Other times, she just entertained me and reminded me of our old friendship and crazy things we'd done together. Sometimes, she would sing rock-a-bye baby and made me sleep. It had been almost twenty years since I was in touch with my old best friends, but that didn't matter to them. I didn't realize until the tragedy how genuinely blessed I was with very loyal friends.

Over several weeks, with the consistent involvement of the friends mentioned above, I slowly started to gain my faith back and decided to go to church. I wasn't ready to return to our former church, which my family had attended the previous twelve years. I wasn't sure I could handle the memory. We loved our church dearly. Through it, we found our church family and made several precious friends with whom we shared our lives, good and bad. Isaiah and I were very active in ministry, and I knew almost everyone by name and considered them all to be my family. One of the plans we had in 2018 was to start going to the English church so we could take our friends who didn't understand Amharic (the language used in our former church) with us. Plus, my son was approaching twelve, and he began to dislike going to the Amharic church. Isaiah mentioned to me his colleague went to a church called Experience Church, and he heard lots of good things about that specific church. We were planning to check it by the end of January. Unfortunately, he passed a week before our appointment. Our couple friends and neighbors, John and Serkadis, took Joseph and Faith to Springs Church during my bereavement months. I knew Springs Church from eleven years prior when they were at McEwen Hall at the University of Calgary. I came across the church when I was studying on campus one Sunday and used to go there every Sunday I went to the campus.

I thanked my friends and took the kids to Experience Church, a great church with very energetic people. The kids loved it, and I loved how they welcomed new people and made us feel comfortable to be involved right away. If it were the old me, I would've jumped in and hit the ground running, but with all I had been going through, I wasn't ready to get involved. Regardless, I thought it wouldn't hurt to check it out more in-depth, so I took their connect courses. I had seen and heard different church politics, so it was quite refreshing to see a church that was willing to welcome a stranger into any position based on your qualification. However, I was not ready to serve. My goal was to heal myself, minimize the pain for my kids, and give them stability.

I was still angry at God, but I knew I needed to keep going to church even when I didn't feel like going. One Sunday, I decided to check out Springs Church again. The people in hospitality were amazing, and their smiles were so encouraging. I loved the worship and darker setting of the room, which allowed me space to cry without being noticed and put off the pressure of having to look my best. I could come wearing my athletic clothing and still worship freely. I felt we needed a home church. While my kids loved Experiences, I'd fallen in love with Springs. So, we kept alternating between the two churches for a few weeks while praying for God's guidance on which one to settle. In a dream, Pastor Leon gave me a book, and while I still don't know what it means, it helped me to decide to call Springs Church home.

One challenging day, a religious lady who was a good friend of Isaiah's called me. She mentioned she was so sad Isaiah decided to go to hell instead of obeying God and serving him with glory. I didn't know what to say, so I wept. My mind was blurry those days, and I couldn't think properly about anything.

When I went to church the next Sunday, Pastor Leon was preaching. I didn't listen to what he was saying because I was busy with the lingering question the lady left in my head: whether Isaiah made it to Heaven or not. I wept throughout the service. After he finished preaching and people started to leave, I ran to the front with tears streaming down my face and asked Pastor Leon if I could hug him. He gave me a very generous hug and said, "Are you ok?" I tried to put myself together, but I was still crying when I told him about the tragedy and asked him, "Is my husband in Heaven?" Without wavering and with confidence, he said, "Absolutely!"

I was a bit shocked by his confident assurance. Pastor Leon continued to explain to me if Christians were in a car accident, where do they go? I said to Heaven. He continued, "How about if they have a heart attack? How about if they have cancer?" He explained addiction is also a sickness. The overdose Isaiah took was to help him cope with whatever pain he was feeling at the moment, and that dependency on the drug was a sickness. I said, "But the Bible said drunkards should not inherit the kingdom of God." He said, "That's a good question. What is the kingdom of God, and where is it?" Without waiting for me to answer, he continued: "The kingdom of God is not a matter of eating and drinking, but of righteousness, peace, and joy in the Holy Spirit. The kingdom of God is now, and here. When people choose to do the right things and allow the Holy Spirit into their lives to guide them, they enjoy their life, and they live in peace and joy here on earth now. However, getting into Heaven is a gift, and it is only received by believing in Jesus Christ. From what you have told me, your husband believed in Jesus Christ, so he is in Heaven. Go in peace and keep coming to church." Pastor Leon's sincere hug and his answer took a heavy load off my heart, and ever since, I've been attending Springs Church and listening to his messages.

Blaming God didn't reduce my pain. The prayers of many people and generous support from loyal friends helped me put God first again in my life. Trusting God and His grace in all ways gave me the courage to live every single day with hope and peace. Amen.

4
FLASHBACKS

Isaiah left a lot of memories in the hearts of hundreds. We treasure several good memories. His deep voice and fast steps made him noticeable in any gatherings. His eloquent speeches were unforgettable by many who got the chance to listen to them. He was very involved in the house and church. Even after our separation, he would come at least once a week to clean the house and cook for us. The main memory of Daddy the kids have is at the dining table. Although I have learned some of his recipes throughout the years, the kids would, at times, say they have missed his beautiful presentation and step in to help.

Unfortunately, I had also been traumatized by several undesirable memories. The dreadful flashbacks I suffered from happened when I would pass through his apartment building, which is next to my office. The day of his passing has played on my mind several times, and before I would get to work, I parked my car in the visitors' parking and cried for a bit. Thanks to God, since I mainly work from home, I didn't have to visit the office often, and after few months, we had opened a new office in a different location to collocate our project team.

The other tormenting flashback I had was when I passed through a building in Southland, where we had gathered with the church elders to intervene with Isaiah's struggles. He didn't stay until the end of the meeting because he had to teach children that evening. However, he promised us he would comply with the recommendations and plan I had put together should he ever fail again. I remember crying a lot during that meeting. I knew if he didn't do something, it would cost us his life, and sadly it did. For me, passing by that building is still very painful.

About ten months after Isaiah's tragic passing, I went to visit my friend's brother at Rocky View Hospital, the same hospital where I gave birth to all my children. After we spent a few minutes exchanging greetings, my friend asked me to share the word of God. We were using our cellphone to read the word of God, but his nurse came and said we couldn't use our cell phone due to the unit policy, so we decided to use the hospital's chapel. The moment I entered the chapel, a special memory came to my mind. When I was pregnant with my second child, the child was overdue, so my doctor decided to induce me. The nurses allowed us to walk around, so Isaiah and I had gone to the chapel to pray. I remembered Isaiah using the piano to worship God while I was praying. That memory overwhelmed me, and I couldn't hold back my tears, so I asked my friend to continue prayer while I tried to control my crying. After the prayers, my friend told me about a person from our community who was in ICU and asked me if I could go with her to visit him. So, we left the chapel and went to the ICU area. We found the family in a waiting room, which was comfortable enough to pray and share some words. As per the request of my friend, I shared some words with them. I don't remember the details of what I have said, but I sensed God comforting me through what I shared with them. God somehow enabled me to pray with them and share the message of hope and strength. I emphasized to them to trust God, for His grace would allow us to pass through any trouble.

After we left the ICU area and said goodbye to my friend, the thoughts of Isaiah's love for people came to mind. He helped people at hospitals, and he would tell me stories about ICU. It was my first time to see someone in ICU . . . how I wished he was with me to explain what was happening. He was fearless and a sacrificial giver, supporter, encourager. He had the gift to show up in a sad situation and change the atmosphere. I sensed I applied what I learned from him. I had felt our presence gave some comfort to the family in their dark moment and a hope to lean on God's grace no matter what the outcome would be. I was proud of myself for meeting some new people and managed to pray and encourage them despite my grief.

Then, an overwhelming thought came to my mind: *would this person survive?* According to his nurse, there wasn't hope, but his sister, who came from the USA, said she believed in God. It reminded me of myself when I was requesting God to raise Isaiah. I was hoping and praying for God to grant her the desires of her heart. On the other side, I was concerned for her if the outcome was different from what she was anticipating. I was overwhelmed with the emotions of the flashback.

The moment I stepped into my car, the following word of God came to my heart:

> Humble yourselves, therefore, under God's mighty hand, that he may lift you up in due time. Cast all your anxiety on him because he cares for you. Be alert and of sober mind. Your enemy, the devil, prowls around like a roaring lion looking for someone to devour. Resist him, standing firm

in the faith, because you know that the family of believers throughout the world is undergoing the same kind of sufferings. (1 Peter 5:6-9, NIV)

I thought I needed to stand by the family and continued to follow up with them. I prepared them for whatever might come on their way. During that time, when I focused on the family, I managed to pray without wetting my eyes, despite the urge. After a few weeks, I heard the person passed away, but I stayed in touch with his sister. I hoped and prayed God's grace would enable the family to pass through the darkness with strength.

One day, another dear friend from our former church insisted I attend a conference, and despite my feelings, I went to make her happy. The moment I stepped into the church, an overwhelming memory came to my mind, and I couldn't hold back my tears. My friends were excited to see me and gave me a warm welcome, but memories of Isaiah's worship dance in such conferences and his funeral played in my mind from the moment I stepped into the venue. I finished the entire service, which lasted about four hours, weeping.

Speaking of Isaiah's worship dance, our church has conferences at least twice a year, and one of the things we remember is Isaiah's unique worship dance. He would lift both his hands as high as he could and dancing before the Lord as if he was alone, regardless of who was watching. I used to call him King David. "And David danced before the Lord" (2 Samuel 6:14-22 [NLT]).

One of my favorite pleasant flashbacks was when I came home from the spa that Saturday night before he died, and he came to spend time with the kids. I found him worshiping with Hill songs (one of our family's favorite worship teams) and dancing with Faith, my middle child, while carrying the youngest one on his shoulder. I'd seen him dancing several times, but that one went for about forty-five minutes, and they were making beautiful moves. I wish I had recorded it, but it's still fresh in my memory. I even sketched about that on worship night and called it the "last worship dance of Isaiah." One day, I will share it with my kids; I know Faith also remembers it because she has reminded me about that evening couple of times.

Overall, I have had different experiences of nightmares and pleasant memories. Through it all, I thank God for His grace, and I have intentionally started creating memories for my family. I would also encourage anyone to do so, as we are all going to pass, but the memories we build will last longer, if not forever.

Part 1: Let Us Reflect

1. Are you actively grieving any kind of loss right now?

2. Are you dealing with any regret?

3. Are you angry at anyone?

4. Do you have any flashbacks?

PART 2
ALLOWING THE
PAIN TO LESSEN

It has been said, "time heals all wounds." I do not agree. The wounds remain. In time, the mind, protecting its sanity, covers them with scar tissue and the pain lessens. But it is never gone.

—Rose Fitzgerald Kennedy

5
FORGIVENESS

Many years ago, I heard a preacher speaking at a women's conference explain unforgiveness is like carrying a rotten potato in your purse wherever you go; it bothers you more than the person who offended you. Ever since I heard that statement, I always check my heart and do everything in my capacity to forgive anyone, no matter how big or small the offense might be. I even have a personal principle to forgive everyone before they offend me; this has helped me let go of lots of grudge and bitterness that could've damaged my health.

One of the main cultures/principles at Springs Church is also forgiveness. Pastor Leon always reminds us to be "unoffendable." I agree with Pastor Leon; when we forgive, we live a healthier life, and the benefit is ours. Honestly, grieving made me very sensitive, and I had to make extra effort to follow the principle of not holding any grudge against anyone.

The hardest part was letting go and letting myself off the hook, as I thought I should've done something to prevent the incident. Plus, I felt I didn't show enough love and respect to him; I was openly disappointed with his addiction and thought he wasn't doing enough to overcome it. I felt like he didn't respect my advice. Regardless, I wish I'd shown him more love and respect. So, the first person I had to forgive was myself for the things I thought I hadn't done to support him.

The second person I needed to forgive was Isaiah himself; God is the only one that can give good judgment. However, I felt he failed his kids and me by not doing whatever it took to solve the problem, which cost us having him in our lives. The choices my husband made not only cost me a great deal while he was alive, but I also needed to deal with lots of messes left behind, including some contentious matters with family members. Well, there's nothing he can do about it now, so I chose to forgive him instead of being bitter about the stuff I needed to address.

The third person I needed to forgive was the building superintendent. Had she allowed us to get into his apartment, perhaps we could've taken Isaiah to the hospital before it was too late. However, after I saw the result of his autopsy, he was dead by the time we arrived, according to their estimate. Regardless, there's no point in being angry at her; she was following her policy, so I forgave her.

After the funeral, one of the people I needed to confront was Isaiah's relative. I thought he didn't handle his arguments with Isaiah wisely and triggered the entire tragic incident. At first, he seemed to be shocked and grieving, but to make matters worse, a couple of days after the funeral, he sent a message via my brother to get his cologne and some cultural spices he'd left at Isaiah's apartment. Oh, God! I was furious! We were grieving a precious life, and he was concerned about his cologne? I didn't even want to see that person again ever! By God's grace, I recently managed to forgive him, and I think I might be ok to see him again in the future.

I'm still angry about the overall health system when it comes to an addicted person's family. As Isaiah mostly functioned as an average person, I couldn't do anything to seek help for him because he took his problem lightly and thought he could overcome it by himself. And when I approached the health system, their answer was they couldn't do anything without his willingness. I see their point: you can't force an adult to choose the right thing. However, my challenge is if addiction is categorized as mental health, we already know that person can't reason out and do what is best for him, so why couldn't the family decide on his behalf? I had a lengthy battle with the system to send Isaiah to at least a one-year rehabilitation center; however, since he thought he didn't need it, nothing could reinforce what would have prevented the death.

The second challenge I had with the health system was the long time it took them to release his autopsy and cause of his death. I didn't have closure for almost a year despite my suspicion, and that had its pain. Regardless, I choose to forgive.

The other group I was furious with is the illegal drug dealers who manipulate the victim for their gain. Whoever made and sold these drugs are not only my enemies but the enemies of many families. However, we can only work on the demand side because it seems no force is competent enough to stop the supply end. I feel the dealers are cruel and have no sympathy for their clients. I don't have any words to describe my emotions towards them, but again, I choose to forgive them.

Our community is gracious. During the first few weeks, I had thousands of visitors, pastors, and community leaders who said what they thought would be helpful. At the time, I was emotionally numb and was not really paying attention to what they said. I felt nothing; all I was waiting for was for everyone to go home so I could try to process everything alone with God. At the same time, after everyone went back to their lives, I became deeply sad and replayed in my mind some of the nonsense preaching indicating the tragedy is God's will. That kind of teaching will never make sense to me. My mind also started to play some of the unhelpful comments some people said. One of them was a comment made by a very close person to Isaiah: "This was not a surprise for me; I was expecting it." It was painful to hear, not helpful at all. A friend also mentioned, "You shouldn't feel sorry for him; he was selfish and irresponsible. You better move on and take care of yourself." Such judgmental comments worsen my pain, but now, by the grace of the Lord, I have forgiven the people who made unnecessary comments unintentionally or intentionally.

One day, I went to a mall to buy a backpack for my daughter. I noticed a hairstylist who used to braid my hair a long time ago. We have known her family for a while, and her husband was very close to us. I was eager to say hello to her, and all of a sudden, after she saw me, she turned around and left in haste, as if she saw a dangerous item. *Oh my! It hurts!* I didn't know it back then, but death and grief make people uncomfortable and react awkwardly. It caused me some pain then, but now I forgive her.

On another occasion, two ladies I knew were walking towards me in our neighborhood, and one of them stopped to say hello, while the other continued her walk and paused to wait for her friend. Then, thinking about how the other person was very close to our family, I thought she didn't recognize me, so I was stupid enough to check. "Don't you recognize me?" She said yes, and I didn't know what to say next; sorrowful and awkward emotions overwhelmed my body. Well, by God's grace, I now forgive.

Overall, the people I thought would be there for me were not there. On the other hand, the people I never expected to do anything became my biggest supporters. One of my biggest supporters, next to my youngest sister, Semhar, was my former manager Judi. She shared with me how she suffered the loss of her mom in her early teens and made herself available for me to lean on her whenever I needed support with the kids. Another person who is still on my support line is Gebremicael Fishatsion, a longtime friend and family member; bless his heart, he has lifted lots of weight from my shoulders. I'm blessed with many supporters.

I want to mention some of my great supporters who live in my neighborhood: Wondesh, Hirut, Simret, Dani, Lina, Serkie, John, Jenn, Andre, and Melanie. They have provided practical support, from cleaning and decorating the house to driving the kids to different occasions—I am forever grateful for their kindness. So, I started to disregard other people's offenses by counting the favor God gave me with my supporters.

If you're struggling with dealing with any offensive things people did or said to you, I would like to encourage you to decide to forgive and say the following prayer with me: "I refuse to harbor anger, grudge, bitterness, and unforgiveness in Jesus' mighty name, Amen!"

6
SELF CARE

I have to admit I wasn't good at taking care of myself. I usually had a hectic schedule—I do enjoy working—and thanks to God, somehow, work seems to keep coming my way. I know God's grace is enabling me to do what I am doing; however, it wouldn't be sustainable if I don't take care of myself. When we're grieving, it's more important than ever to take care of ourselves. Sometimes, people who are very good at taking care of others are not good at taking care of themselves. The stress of a significant loss can quickly deplete energy and emotional reserves. Looking after our physical and emotional needs will help us get through difficult times.

My personal coach once suggested, "Simret, you must face your feelings." She knew I was trying to suppress my grief, but we both knew I couldn't avoid it forever. To lessen the pain, I had to first acknowledge the pain. Trying to avoid feelings of sadness and loss only prolongs the grieving process. If we don't deal with it properly, the pain could lead our life to a darker pit hole. As per the article medically reviewed by Stephanie Hariston that I read on the Recovery Village site, unresolved grief can also lead to depression, anxiety, substance abuse, and health problems. So, we must take care of ourselves as we grieve. Even though practicing self-care wasn't always easy for me, I have become intentional lately and continue to juggle my priorities on purpose.

I am sharing below some suggestions based on my personal experience. I am not writing this book as an expert but as an ordinary person who loves to share her heart in the hope of supporting others. So, please take what you like and discard the rest.

6.1 Spiritual Care

It took me a while to regain my confidence in prayer and nurture my spirit being while grieving. However, I had several spiritual encounters in my life, and I can't deny God's existence. I understand life isn't easy, and it has fierce storms. I know by building my life on Christ, the solid rock is the only thing that would help me sustain. Our beloved Pastor Leon says, "The storms don't make the house strong, it comes to destroy it, but the builder who builds the house on a solid foundation helps the house to overcome the storm."

I have not only believed in God as the creator of the universe, but I have also decided to build my life in Him and on His word. The time I invested in the good times to build my spiritual life helped me sustain during the difficulties, and I'm slowly gaining my strength back. I now strive daily to learn His instructions and plans for my life. I've been experiencing God as a gentle Father and friend and a strong shield and protector against my enemies. According to Jeremiah 29:11 (NIV), His plans are there to prosper me and not to harm me; they're plans to give me hope and a future. I wouldn't be writing this book if God wasn't in me and with me.

Reading this book, you might not believe in God or the spiritual realm; I respect that. For me, God is real, and there is a spiritual realm. Life has shown me its ugly face, and I have gone through many shadows of death, which are hard and scary. I have also self-imposed pain by making unwise decisions. However, God's grace enabled me to walk through them. So, for me, I would like to invest first in my spiritual strength. I'm doing whatever it takes to maintain my spiritual health by scheduling time to study God's word and pray. Amid the difficulty, I trust God can use the misfortunes for His purpose.

Let me share some of my favourite verses that I have been meditating on this morning below. I want to invite you to read them aloud and meditate on them for a few minutes too: "I will instruct you and teach you in the way you should go; I will counsel you with my loving eye on you" (Psalm 32:8, NIV).

"Trust in the Lord with all your heart and lean not on your own understanding; in all your ways submit to him, and he will make your paths straight" (Proverbs 3:5-6 , NIV).

"Whether you turn to the right or to the left, your ears will hear a voice behind you, saying, 'This is the way; walk in it'" (Isaiah 30:21, NIV).

I've never heard an audible voice from God, but since I've accepted God as my Lord, Father, and leader, He was faithful in leading me throughout my life using a way that's clear to me. There was a time when I didn't want to do what God wanted me to do, and the consequences were horrible. The good thing is God is always a God of another chance. He's not like human beings. The moment I call Him for help, He is there. He gave me chance after chance while I was becoming stronger from several dark situations.

I consider myself spiritual, and one way I take care of my spiritual health is by investing more time to get to know the Creator, God. I can't stop talking about my relationship with God and what He has done in my life. I'm always eager to increase my knowledge of Him and allow His principles to guide my paths in whatever situation. I declare His divine protection and its continuous supply throughout my life. His favor and grace are my prime tools to prevail against all the odds I have faced and might face in the future.

I encourage you to make God first in your life too; you have nothing to lose. God doesn't force you to accept or follow Him; however, if you choose to invite Him into your life and take His guidance, you'll have peace that surpasses understanding in any circumstances. As a beneficiary of His presence in my life, I would like to encourage you to invite Him into your life right now. Why wait?

6.2 Physical Care

The second thing I decided to do was to look after my physical health. I decided to eat healthily and exercise regularly. My family and friends would tell you I say there are two places I would never regret going: church and the gym. With the COVID-19 lockdown, both had to be done remotely, so I decided to invest in the equipment I need to maintain my physical health.

If I had unlimited time and resources on my hand, I think I would devote myself to spiritual and physical care. I would love to inspire grieving people to get physically healthy. The mind and body are connected. When you feel physically healthy, you'll be better able to cope emotionally and spiritually.

I know when you're grieving, getting out and being physically active might be the last thing you feel like doing; however, we need to subdue our feelings and stick with doing the right thing. Exercises don't only allow us to stimulate our body health; it also contributes to our emotional health. Let's combat the emotional stress and fatigue of grieving by eating right and exercising regularly.

6.3 Sleeping

The third area of self-care I worked on was getting regular sleep. I'm usually a good sleeper; however, after Isaiah's tragic death, sleeping was one of the areas where I struggled. It also added up when the kids woke me in the middle of the night. My sleeping pattern was disrupted for some time. Thanks to God and the prayers from my friends, I'm finally getting better at sleeping.

I've also done my part by adjusting my evening routines, such as eliminating caffeine from my diet, spending a few minutes on reflection, and following a consistent sleeping time. I can sense my energy is higher when I get enough sleep, and I thank God for the good nights of sleep. I should also give some credit to my chamomile tea; it's one of my favorite evening drinks, and it works its magic. Getting enough sleep is crucial.

6.4 Personal Development

Personal growth is the fourth area that I'm investing in. I love learning, and I don't think I'll ever stop learning. I'm a big dreamer, and I need discipline to develop myself so I can achieve my dreams. I'm continually investing in expanding my capacity to solve problems at a new level. I listen to audiobooks, take courses, and work on elevating myself to the next level, whether on my parenting, day job, or businesses.

Personal development has been an excellent way of distracting myself from the negative emotions of grief in a positive way. I have made a conscious effort to learn more in the past couple of years in leadership, life skills, and effective parenting, which has helped me enhance the quality of my coaching to my kids and clients. It also helped me to analyze my core values and discover my identity.

6.5 Entertainment

One of my weaknesses is not spending enough time on leisure activities. I blame my late father for this, as he was a workaholic and believed entertainment was for lazy people. Even though he was a reasonably wealthy man, he never approved any of my budget requests for entertainment. Of course, the situation back home wasn't conducive to relaxation. However, I used to be jealous of people who would take some time to entertain themselves.

I always wanted my parents to take us for a vacation to Massawa, a beautiful coastal city in Eritrea, not very far from Asmara, the city we lived. Often, I would politely suggest to my dad our family needed to take some breaks and enjoy life within the domain of what was doable there and then. He would always answer my requests by saying, "We are here on earth to work hard to make the world a better place, not to enjoy life." Even though I disagreed with my dad, somehow, that upbringing influenced me, and I still find myself struggling to justify spending any time on entertainment. I'm still not knowledgeable in the entertainment industry. I have very minimal knowledge of Hollywood stars and television icons; however, I watch a few movies here and there. I love travelling and spending time with nature. Since my son complained some work is always attached to my travels, I plan to schedule some trips with my kids with no business in it.

From my experience, when grieving, you sometimes feel guilty when you take care of yourself, especially when you consider the physical body of your loved one is decaying. However, you're still here, and you can't fulfill your purpose in life if you don't take care of your body. Our physical body is our vehicle to function on earth. Plus, we won't add any value to the late loved one by not taking care of ourselves; we would only minimize the value of the life we ought to live. So, if you are grieving, I encourage you to take good care of yourself.

Some people use alcohol or drugs to numb the pain of grief or lift their mood artificially; however, I don't recommend it because it may lead to a darker path. Nothing we do in the future will change our love for the person who died. Eventually, we'll have to rerun our life. Perhaps you'll date again, have another child, seek new experiences, etc. None of these things will diminish your love for the person you lost.

On the other hand, I believe the person who died would be proud of you for taking care of yourself. There are several books and online tips on self-care. If you don't know where to start, check an excellent article by Tchiki Davis, Ph.D., titled "Self-Care: 12 Ways to Take Better Care of Yourself." The report also includes a link to self-care strategies and a well-being quiz that can help you learn which self-care strategies may help you.

7
CARE FOR OTHERS

Isaiah and I had a lot of differences, and it seemed we were from the opposite spectrum of personality (Hey! Opposites attract!). Despite our differences, one of the things we had in common from day one was our love for people and the joy we had for helping others without expecting anything in return. Isaiah's act of kindness to others was second to none. Without exaggeration, sometimes, he was volunteering about forty hours per week. He helped many refugees settle and be familiar with Canadian culture. He was committed to our church, volunteering in different areas, and volunteered at AWANA (Children's Bible study program) for a couple of years. He visited people in hospitals and prisons to spread God's word. Even though it's not at Isaiah's level of commitment, loving people and helping others comes naturally to me too.

My desire to support others was what led me to marry Isaiah. He was a person with excellent qualities and potentials but struggling in some areas of his life. He was very open about his challenges; however, I thought it was history. I didn't know much about addiction or relapse back then. I was new to Canada and a very naive Christian. I thought prayers could solve everything; I thought God and I would get to Isaiah's world and rescue him. I endured a lot of pain in the process, and things didn't go the way I expected. However, I've learned a lot from the experience, and I have no regret about the choice I made. Isaiah was worth knowing and having a family with; even though they were very few years, I treasure his great memories. I also learned from him how to support others effectively. Somehow, it didn't work on him, but he had a pearl of great wisdom on rescuing and lifting others from the mud.

I would be lying if I said I enjoyed everything about my married life. I endured lots of sorrow, including the tragic death. However, lately, I discovered the challenges I went through shaped my life and helped me gain resilience. I wouldn't be as resilient and unshakable without those experiences. If you allow God to intervene, adversities can shape you, make you strong, and equip you to help others more. I'm not perfect; I have many weaknesses, and I wish I had a smooth ride in life.My challenges in life helped me make myself always available to support others as much as I can. When you grieve, you feel you are at the receiving end, and you want others to help you; however, I found out healing begins when you get up and take care of others.

The primary focus of my care is my children. They all have reacted differently to the tragedy. So, I needed to take intentional time to monitor each of them and respond to their questions. Not too long ago, we picked up my daughter's friend for a play date, and they started chitchatting. Her friend said, "2020 is the worst year ever; I haven't seen my friends in four months. I hope 2021 will be a better year." My daughter responded, "No, 2018 was the saddest year because my dad died. I haven't seen my dad for almost three years now."

I pretended I didn't hear anything, but later that evening, I needed to take my daughter for a walk and let her talk it out more. I realized she got jealous when she saw her friends play with their dads. She told me how she enjoyed it when Isaiah had taken her to Starbucks and bought her steamed milk and almond biscuit.

The next day after work, I was tired and wished to sleep, but I thought taking care of her emotional need took precedence. So, I tried my best to spend some more time with her. We played some board games and made her favorite hot chocolate. Since Isaiah's passing, I've had to drop several things to be there for my children. I have declined pleasant job offers that demanded more of my time and have decided to stay working from home to get more time with my children and supervise their activities. At times, it's very taxing to take care of three kids with three different personalities. However, I do it intentionally and joyfully with the grace of God. I would like to be a faithful steward of the gifts of my children's lives and prepare them for their future. Despite the sacrifices, it gives me joy to take care of my children.

I am humbled to say I knew almost everyone by name in our former church, even though it's a reasonably sized one. I was active in several ministry activities, from coordinating different fundraising events to teaching the word of God. However, I most enjoyed mentoring and coaching individuals within my former church. The interaction with individuals allowed me to know several people, pray with them, and encourage them. When I came to a new church, I lost most of my connections. Due to the limitation of time and capacity, I couldn't see my old friends as often, but I'm sure we would hit it off if we got a chance to meet with each other again. The rapport I built for more than ten years in my former church is not in vain; I know for sure we are in each other's hearts forever. By God's grace, I continued mentoring a few young people from there and have seen my mentees heading upward to fulfill their dreams—this has been a source of energy for me.

I realized I needed to start building relationships in our new church, Springs Church. Most of the people at Springs Church are friendly, and if I put my mind to it, I believe it wouldn't take long before I made some good friends. Within a few months of going to Springs, they announced a summer camp. When we'd go camping before, we would always have a cabin, and Isaiah would take care of the rest. All I had to do was pack my items and go. I thought it would be a great way to build some friendships. I signed to go and offered to take my new immigrant friend's two teenagers. The teens were super excited because they hadn't left Calgary since arriving from abroad. The camp organizer told me there were no cabins available, and my options were to rent a trailer or bring my tent. I had been to several remote areas for fieldwork doing some site assessments. However, I would always travel to the closest town and sleep in a hotel. I had never slept in the open-air, and it had been a while since I pitched a tent, so I realized renting a trailer would be a better option. The good thing was the rental company drove the trailer to the campground and set up everything for us. I thought it would be an excellent opportunity to spend some time with the kids and get them away from electronics. However, I ran out of space to pack enough items; after we packed our blankets and some food, the SUV had no room left. I went to the campground with five kids. After all, I thought it was a church camp, and I hoped someone would step in if I was in trouble.

The trailer was great; it has all the necessary kitchen items, and I had done some research for do's and don'ts, so the first day was fun. On day two, I discovered I wasn't ready to prepare food for five kids every day (three of them teenagers). The food I thought would last a week was gone by the end of the second day. I didn't want the kids to notice, but I said to myself, *Maybe this is beyond my capacity; we should go back home*. I tried to think of a way to break the news to the teens when they came back to the trailer from their exploration around the camp. When I saw them coming, my little ones jumped all over them, and they were all smiling and full of joy. When I saw the excitement on the kiddos' faces, I decided to go grocery shopping at a nearby place without them noticing. The following morning, I bought whatever edible items I could find, such as milk, bread, hotdogs, etc., and with the blessings of God, we made it through the week.

The kids had a blast, but I didn't personally enjoy the camping; not only was I exhausted taking care of the kids, but also, I felt so lonely, and it made me miss Isaiah and my former church. The families there knew each other; they were having fun together and inviting themselves to each other's cabin while I was grieving my loneliness. It was very different from going to camp with my former church family. I would be the one enjoying it the most. I also realized our culture of hospitality and taking care of a guest is a bit different. I tried my best to go beyond my negative emotions and managed to make a few friends, but it was not my favorite camping experience, for sure. Thank God we made it home safely; I got to know some people, and it had left something good in the kids' memory. My first act of kindness after the loss was taking those teens to camp with me, and they always remember it, so I didn't regret it.

Being a doer, I didn't sit and do nothing for long at Springs Church. I gladly attended the connect courses that were a prerequisite for volunteering and selected a couple of areas where I felt I could contribute, given my limited availability. Then, the kids' church leader contacted me and said they needed help. I was pleased because I thought that would give me some more time to spend with my kids. The diverse volunteers and leaders of the kids' church at Springs are some of the best. I happily took the required courses, got my police clearance, and started volunteering where they needed the most help: Nursery 2. The toddlers required a lot of energy. Despite it being a bit challenging, by the grace of the Lord, I'm still serving. My wish is for other churches to give the same priorities to kids. I reached out to Sunday school ministry leaders who I knew and shared my experiences at Springs with them. I encouraged them to structure the kids' ministry in a way to minister to the kids. In some churches, kids are babysat, and they're not considered a priority; therefore, they get easily bored, and by the age of twelve, they don't want to go to church. My son was already starting to say he didn't want to go to church at age eleven because he felt he didn't have much to do. His Sunday school teacher was trying her best to engage him, but it wasn't enough. At Springs, he's not only enjoying going to church but also volunteering at church with me. That's one of my biggest wins. What I have learned is when the kids' ministry is given priority and run effectively, the older kids could be part of it. It's such a great blessing to see our kids learning and thriving. Thank you, kids church and volunteers at Springs family.

I would like my kids to learn about their origin and be as proud of their biological identity as they are of their spiritual identity. Every Saturday, I take them to the Eritrean Language and Cultural School in Calgary. Volunteers run the school, and when I realized they needed help, I began helping in whatever area I could while I waited for the kids to finish their classes. Soon after, they selected me to join the board, and the board elected me as the principal of the school. Of course, the appointment came with its demand for responsibility, and I have to devote some time to work with the teachers, board members, and volunteers. However, it's worth the effort; we are very blessed with amazing fathers and mothers who would work relentlessly to equip our children with a good culture and a language we have inherited from our fathers. The number of our students is growing, and it has been a source of friendship and fellowship for both the parents and the kids. I'm very humbled and proud to be part of it.

I know I can't run in full capacity to help others, but I'm always mindful of doing what I can to support any need that comes to my attention. I'm a firm believer that giving rewards you better than receiving, and we should never be tired of taking care of others. If you are grieving a loss right now, I highly encourage you to volunteer somewhere, be involved in community services, and take care of others. It might accelerate your healing—give it a try.

When we live on purpose to love and support others, it always rewards us internally. There's a gift and talent in you that can benefit someone around you. Get out of your comfort zone and do something good for someone. Here's one of my experiences I have documented in my journal from the winter of 2019:

Get out of your pity party and reach out

I am writing this unintentionally as God has showered me with joy after I have done a simple act of kindness. It is a long weekend, and I wanted to catch up with some house chores and invited my old friend over. I haven't seen my friend, who just immigrated to Canada with her kids, for the past twenty years. She told me her husband lived here for some time, and he drives, so I have assumed they will come, we will have a good time, and I will catch up to my chores. I have soon realized my friend's husband had to work, and I need to give her a ride. She was not living close by; it was a very long drive on a snowy day. I usually enjoy driving, but not when it snows badly like today. Regardless, I was so determined to welcome my friend and her kids to the beautiful city of Calgary. I know it would also be enjoyable for her and me to catch up with each other. So, I decided to pick her up, take her to Springs Church, and bring her home. We ate lunch, our kids had fun, and it was a great day. Physically, I was tired; however, as soon as I drove away from their apartment building after I dropped them in the evening, a joyful feeling spread throughout my being: joy and an unspeakable-wow. A simple act of kindness can reward you with a joy you can't even explain fully. I should do this more. I have had enough excuses to cancel the appointment and curl up in the bed with my girls the entire day; however, I would have missed that encounter of joy!

From now on, I am determined to get out of my pity party and take care of others. I encourage you to do the same. If you are depressed or grieving, get out of your pity party, drop all your excuses, and try to do a simple act of kindness to someone. It is challenging to take care of someone else while you are going through your own storm; however, it's worth it!

Part 2: Let Us Reflect

5. In your diary or on a piece of paper, list the individuals, organizations, and systems you need to forgive.

6. List the individuals, organizations, and systems that you need to ask for forgiveness.

7. How are you taking care of yourself?

8. Are you eating healthy?

9. Are you drinking water?

10. Are you getting enough sleep?

11. Are you regularly working out?

12. Did you go out for a walk and take some fresh air?

PART 3
MOVING
FORWARD

Life is like riding a bicycle. To keep your balance, you must keep moving.

—Albert Einstein

8
MOVE FORWARD
ONE STEP AT A TIME

One of the most horrible feelings of grief was the feeling of being stuck. After what I hoped for was completely shattered, I didn't know what to do next. In general, I lost the appetite to do life again. To make matters worse, I had to deal with a lot of messes left by my husband. The only thing that kept me going the first few months was to care for my children. A few months after the tragedy, my dear friend and neighbor John brought me a grief share brochure from Springs Church, and he encouraged me to attend. Thanks to his recommendation, the grief share program I attended at Springs Church helped me put things into perspective. Most of the participants were grieving the loss of their loved ones for at least a year. I felt I was the only one with a fresh wound, given I joined the program a few months after the tragedy. It was uncomfortable for me to participate in the discussions. I preferred to sit at the back alone so no one would notice and finished almost every session crying. In the first few weeks, I thought I wouldn't get any help from the program and thought I needed to wait for at least a year to benefit from it. However, as a project manager, I wanted to manage the awful feelings of grief in the shortest possible way, so I kept dragging myself there week after week.

At first, I found it more and more depressing to listen to conversations about more deaths. Several weeks into the program, I wasn't fully engaged; it seemed I went there to cry more. However, with the support and prayers from Pastor Patrick, who was the facilitator of the sessions, and the other participants, slowly, I started to open up and pushed myself to be fully engaged. I learned the deep sadness and depression I was feeling at that moment was normal. People shared their experiences, including some of the same awkward encounters I faced during the process; that also helped me understand nothing was wrong with me. The group gave me some tips on how to manage life during the intensive grieving period. At some point, I was still thinking of quitting the sessions because I didn't relate to the grief stories shared; however, I kept dragging myself every Tuesday evening and finished the entire program. Towards the end of the program, there was a message from our pastor, Leon Fontaine, about Heaven. I'm so grateful I didn't quit the program before I heard that message. That specific message was an eye-opener for me and helped me tremendously.

Pastor Leon's message was very comforting in that he didn't diminish the unique pain we were dealing with the loss. He said, "You need to remember when you ask the question of 'why did this happen?' you become judgmental, and the answer you would get would be a guess." He also grabbed my attention when he said how people misquote scriptures and take them out of context. His message made me realize the unexpected loss was not God's intention, nor was it my fault, but the enemy's work. Above all, what gave me a new perspective about death was his explanation about Heaven. I realized how we often forget Heaven is a place of joy and peace. He continued to explain our loved ones were no longer suffering there but rejoicing. It's the perfect place where anyone can be—perfect in peace, perfect in joy, perfect in safety. There's no sickness; there's no sorrow; there's no pain.

After listening to our pastor's message, I couldn't help but smile about Heaven. Pastor Leon's message was given in a video set. However, I didn't want to wait to order the video, so I recorded it on my cellphone and immediately sent it to Isaiah's sisters. They told me it helped them too. As a believer, that specific message made me not be afraid of death anymore. I knew and thought about Heaven before. However, Pastor Leon's message challenged me to believe what I knew and live my belief more tangibly. When I got home that night, I remember confronting death in my room. I said, "'Death,' to tell you the truth, you didn't conquer. Isaiah believed in Christ as his savior, and he is living in Heaven, which is the most perfect place in the entire universe. He is safe with his heavenly Father." I felt some relief after I said those words, and I have decided to accept what I can't change.

Different people grieve at a different pace. I would like to put a timeframe on grieving, but it doesn't work that way. I know I may never entirely move on; it may take my mind years to gather the details and process the whole extent of the loss. Some people thought I should quickly move on, given the hardship imposed on me by Isaiah's lifestyle. They suggested his death would get some relief from dealing with some of the ugly stuff caused by Isaiah's addiction. However, for me, it felt I suffered in vain because I didn't see the fruit of my labor. It made me sad how some people thought, but I know if I didn't help me, no one would. I realized even after my spirit was lifted from the messages I heard on the grief share sessions, it wasn't easy to move on from grieving. Such programs help you to gain some strength and focus. However, they don't have a magic way to have you ultimately move on. I knew I would grieve to some extent at different times, and that was ok.

The concept of moving forward I learned during the grief share made sense to me; however, it took me a while to figure out the first step. After a while, I started by first imagining what would be more valuable: to stay stuck or move forward slowly, one step at a time. The idea of writing this book was part of that moving forward process. I didn't want grief to withhold me from contributing toward the bright future of my children. I decided to focus on living for a moment; life is a collection of hours and days. There will be moments that have their aspect of emptiness. However, there will also be moments full of meanings. There will be moments of sorrow, and there will be moments of joy. I said to myself: *I need to be mindful of cherishing the moment without torturing myself about the past and worrying about the future.* Paying attention and being aware of the moment is the first step I took moving forward.

According to 2 Peter 1:3 (NLT), "By His divine power, God has given us everything we need for living a godly life through the knowledge of Him who called us to His own glory and excellence." Sometimes, we look for comfort to come from someone or somewhere; however, as a believer, I found the best comfort was when I looked inside. God has given me everything I need to comfort myself and others if I take the initiative by taking one step at a time; small steps can make a big difference. My task is to be attentive when the messages of mind and memory come, let my resistance surrender, be calm in my soul, and process it according to the will of the Healer and make myself available for healing. If you want to make progress on your healing, you will need to stop listening to your feelings and allow the Holy Spirit, who lives inside you, to do His work. Even though entirely moving on from grief seems near to impossible, moving forward in life is vital if you want to make progress, and God's grace is available for that.

Isaiah once said while he was teaching a Bible study in our house, "What happened in the past might not be long-forgotten, but it is GONE. We can't change it. Forgive yourself, leave the past behind, and focus on your present moment. Move forward one step at a time!"

9
GRATEFULNESS

Many people shared their wisdom with me during the bereavement period, but one of the most memorable was a lesson my dear friend Roti shared with me about praising God as a sacrifice. He shared a message based on Hebrews 13:15 (KJV): "By him, therefore let us offer the sacrifice of praise to God continually, that is, the fruit of our lips giving thanks to his name." He explained that giving thanks to God when everything is going well is very easy. However, when we maintain the thanksgiving attitude in the middle of a storm and praise God while our heart is broken, it's honored as a sacrifice. It's hard to praise God during a loss. I didn't feel like it for a while; however, giving thanks as a sacrifice made sense.

I'm very grateful to God for taking care of me from the day I was born to the present, and for the future He has planned for my life. God has been faithful to me even when I wasn't faithful to Him. He would guide me on my way out even after I refused to listen to Him and got myself into trouble.

Throughout my grieving, His gentle whisper was always in my heart, and I could sense the warmth of His presence even when I was angry with Him. I'm so grateful for waking up most days with encouraging songs in my heart and mind. God is my all-in-all, and I'm so thankful for being privileged to know Him. I believe it's a privilege to know God and have a personal acquaintance with Him. Many educated and wealthy people still don't know Him. He has been my friend in my loneliest hours and my strength in my weakest. He's my light in the darkness. He's my comfort in my sadness. Thank you, God!

I'm also grateful to God for giving me spiritual families wherever I go. My siblings often say, if someone needs anything from anywhere, Simret would know someone to talk to. They're right; I love people, and I'm blessed to know lots of godly people in most parts of the world. One of the comforting things I noticed during my grief was I have a considerable pool of friends. I'm very grateful for their encouraging messages, prayers, and phone calls from almost every continent. I'm also very appreciative of our Eritrean and Ethiopian communities in Calgary, especially my GFMM family, who served our mourning guests relentlessly for a few weeks. I don't know what I would've done without them. I pray for God to bless them abundantly in every area of their lives.

I once heard someone say the greatest tribute to the dead is not grief but gratitude. In the sadness, somehow, God has given us inner strength and the ability to rejoice in the life we shared. In almost every culture, people remember and speak highly of the deceased. I wish we could've shared that appreciation with them while they were alive. Nonetheless, it's better to celebrate the good memories than destroy ourselves with the sadness of the loss.

I was born and raised in a war zone, witnessed several deaths, and grieved a lot in my lifetime. In my childhood, I noticed our neighbours from the middle part of Ethiopia grieved a bit differently. When their loved one passed during the war, I witnessed some of the wives and mothers hit their chest with a stone until it bled, shaved their hair, and dressed in complete black to mourn for an extended period. Whereas in the Eritrean cultures, the women woke up every morning for a mourning chant that lasted between twelve to forty days. Both the Ethiopian and Eritrean cultures I am familiar with are harsh on the grieving person; the grievers are not only in deep pain from the loss, but they bear the extra burden of proving they're hurting to others. They aren't even allowed to play music; they're expected to be sad.

Isaiah and I used to discuss that culture and reminded ourselves we should celebrate the memory and not harm ourselves during the grieving period. Isaiah was very prescriptive about what he wished would happen at his funeral if he passed away ahead of me. When I shared with friends and family how we were running the memorial service, some were uncomfortable. However, they honored my request, and I'm grateful to them. Later on, I heard some sarcasm and insults from a few people who thought I was trying to be a 'Ferengi'—a 'white person'—but I didn't let that bother me. I was grateful for our GFMM family and the ministers who came from different churches to pray, sing, and share God's word with the family and friends almost every day for two weeks. I'm filled with so much gratitude for so many people in my life, especially our church women for their relentless service. I could've written an entire book talking about each individual and their acts of kindness. For now, I have selected a few so we can learn from them, and hopefully, it will inspire us to do the same.

After a few months, when my family started the new normal, my sister called me and said, "Don't cook anything for supper. There's a lady you haven't met before who would like to bring the kids supper." That evening, a woman named Genet (Geni) arrived at my home with about eight types of food in a special thermos. She introduced herself and said she would set up dinner for the family that evening. She's a fantastic chef, and the presentation was terrific. Not only did she feed our family that evening, but we put the leftovers into the freezer, and I didn't have to cook for about a week. Geni had lost her son a couple of years prior, and she was determined to support anyone grieving. She encouraged me to stay healthy and shared her own story of grief. Since that evening, we've become friends. We talk over the phone and have met a few times; we have shared some tears and laughter. One of the things Geni instilled in my heart was gratitude and lifting others. Her smile is magnetic, and later, I discovered she's known for her generosity in our community. May God raise many Geni's who comfort others with no strings attached.

One time, my mom said, "It's better to have a good neighbor than a good brother who lives far away." I'm blessed with excellent neighbours. Notably, the effort of one family, Mimi and Wondesh, is second to none. For the last three years, this couple has been there for me with their down-to-earth attitudes. They don't say much, just show kindness and goodness when they see an opportunity to do so—I've seen God in their lives. I'm very grateful for all their good deeds, from tirelessly taking my kids to the school bus every morning to shoveling the snow and fixing a clogged toilet. They always check if something needs to be taken care of, and then they take care of it. Sometimes, Wondesh would see something around the house that needed to be adjusted before I saw it, and he would fix it. Then, I would find out from my kids he'd done it. Mimi and Wondesh are genuinely an effulgence of God. I'm so blessed to have them in my life. Their good deeds will remain on my wall of fame forever!

Christmas was Isaiah's favorite holiday. He would decorate the house inside out, cook special meals, invite friends, and host dinners for newcomers. The first Christmas after his death, my son and I managed to stand up the Christmas tree, but we didn't even dare to think about hanging the lights outside. We weren't in the mood, and it felt a bit depressing. To make matters worse, a friend posted how her friends surprised her by decorating their house while she was away. I was honestly happy for her, but it made me feel, well, I didn't think my friends would stretch that much. I was wrong! The next day, my dear friends and neighbors, Serkie and John, called and asked me if I would be home over the weekend. I said yes, and they said they would like to come and set up the outside lights. I was speechless. Since then, every Christmas, John has kindly added it to his to-do list; he would even buy any extra items required, so the house was decorated. Serkie and John are my go-to couple when I need any assistance or prayers. I'm blessed to have them in my life and am forever grateful for their kindness. Being grateful intentionally helps our mind focus on positive energy and reminds us to cherish our family and friends' lives. Let's show gratitude to each other.

Another learning event for me was when a friend called me to check on how things were going. After we chatted for a bit, she started complaining about how busy she was and how her husband didn't help her at home. I usually try to listen patiently; however, that day, I didn't have much time and couldn't have her go on and on with her gripes.

I interrupted her with an apology and said, "Listen, there's a saying in my country 'አቦ ዘላም ዝበከ.'ስ ነቦ ዘይብሉ ከብከ.'" The closest translation I could find was a quote from unknown source that says, "When life gives you every reason to be negative, think of all the reasons to be positive. There's always someone who has it worse." I explained to her, "You need to be sensitive to my situation. I'm fully responsible for raising my three kids, and I'm running a very complex project and have lots of other side hustles, so I'm not the right person to listen to your rant. Besides, I want to encourage you to count your blessings and be thankful because your husband is a very responsible husband and dad; he works hard so you can stay home and raise your kids. I wish I could be fully committed to clean the house and take care of my children at this moment.

One of my regrets in life is I didn't appreciate Isaiah enough because I was so focused on the things he wasn't doing right, and my chance of enjoying him is gone. Life is short, and I recommend you appreciate and value the people around you regardless of their weaknesses."

Then it was dead silent for a good minute. Finally, I said, "Are you there?" She said, "Yes, I'm very sorry. Sometimes, we take things for granted, and you're right; I shouldn't have complained to you."

I said, "No problem," and we hung up. I know there are bad days in life; however, I encourage us to count our blessings and be grateful for what we have.

Learn to give thanks always for all things. It makes no difference if you're grieving or going through difficulties. Irrespective of such challenges, don't forget to offer a sacrifice of thanksgiving. The Bible states that giving thanks in all things is the will of God in Christ Jesus concerning our lives. (1 Thessalonians 5:8, NIV) Let's have the thanksgiving attitude; consciously count our blessings and be grateful.

Part 3: Let Us Reflect

13. Are you stuck in any situation?

14. What is the very next step you can take forward?

15. List the individuals, organizations, and systems that you are grateful for.

PART 4
HELPING A
GRIEVING
PERSON

It's the process of grieving that's important and necessary, not the understanding of it.

—Unknown

10
FACTS ABOUT GRIEF AND GRIEVING

On November 4, 2020, a horrible war started in Northern Ethiopia around the border of Eritrea. I was heartbroken, as a war personally costs me lots of lives; my beloved uncles, cousins, neighbours, and friends. The battle is still going as I write this paragraph, and it is deplorable to realize thousands of families will mourn their loved ones. The coronavirus-2019 (COVID19) pandemic also caused about 2.2 Million deaths, as per the World Health Organization website report as of February 2, 2021.

According to the Disease Control and Prevention (CDC), 2.8 resident deaths were registered in the United States in 2018; according to Statistics Canada, there were about 0.3 million deaths in the same year in Canada. When I read these statistics, my heart went out to grieving people following the deaths. In this part of the world alone, if we assume, there are on average of four grievers per loss, which means every year, there are approximately 12.4 million broken-hearted grievers.

It's hard to know what to expect during the grieving process. It is important for me to read on the subject and do more research to help me navigate through my journey and support others. Despite my experiences with several losses, I never took the time to understand grief before. Nor did I learn the facts about grieving until I decided to put my experiences on paper out of a strong desire to give some comfort, direction, and hope to my children and myself.

Most of the advice, such as forgiveness, maintaining a grateful attitude, and helping others, agrees with the Bible's facts, which confirms the Bible is never outdated. I have been the prime beneficiary of my research, and I pray this book will assist and comfort people in the early, numbing days of loss and help them understand what to expect in the months that follow. In Eritrea, it's not common to have formal counselling during grief; however, our communities support each other. Fortunately, we have brought that culture with us. I have received tremendous support from the Eritrean Canadian Community Association of Calgary (ECCAC), especially during the first few weeks of the tragic loss. I can't emphasize enough how much community support plays a beneficial role in supporting a grieving person.

I thank God for the resources we have around in this part of the world. Despite the generous support from my community and church, I have also decided to see a counsellor as I started to get depressed a few weeks after the incident. On my first appointment, the counsellor asked me, "Do you know the stages of grief?" I had no clue, but his question created curiosity, and I did my research to find out what he was talking about. Grief is very personal, and it doesn't follow any linear steps. However, in 1969, a Swiss-American psychiatrist named Elizabeth Kübler-Ross wrote in her book *"On Death and Dying"* that grief could be divided into five stages, which are widely adopted. You can read her book to learn more; however, I have listed below the grief stages that I have gone through.

Stage 1: Shock and Denial

Grief is an overwhelming emotion. It's common to respond to the intense and often sudden feelings by pretending the loss or change isn't happening. It's a common defense mechanism and helps numb us to the intensity of the situation. The first couple of days, although I have now acknowledged the facts, I didn't believe it. I didn't accept the news, and I felt my husband Isaiah would rise when we went to pray over his body. I thought I was applying the word of God and my faith, but now, I realize I was in disbelief and denial.

Denying it gave me some time to absorb the news and begin to process it more gradually. As I moved out of the denial stage, however, the emotions I was hiding began to arise. I was confronted with much sorrow I'd denied; the feelings were profound.

Stage 2: Anger

Anger can hide many of the emotions and pain we carry. Where denial may be considered a coping mechanism, anger is a masking effect. This anger may be redirected toward other people, such as the person who died, our ex, or our old boss. We may even aim our anger at inanimate objects. While our rational brain knows the object of our anger isn't to blame, our feelings in that moment are too intense to understand that. Anger may mask itself in emotions like bitterness or resentment. I shared earlier my experience of being angry at people and God, and honestly, during those moments of my disgrace, I didn't realize it was part of the grieving process. I thought I was losing it. As the anger subsided, I began to think more rationally about what was happening and felt the emotions I'd pushed aside.

Stage 3: Guilt and Pain

During grief, we may feel vulnerable and helpless. In those moments of intense emotions, it's common to experience feelings of pain, sadness, and remorse. We may find ourselves creating a lot of "what if" and "if only" statements. I've had lots of "what if" and "if only" views. I felt like I could have done something to prevent Isaiah's death. I felt regret from not being able to persuade him enough to get admitted into rehab, and at times, I counted all the flaws of my life and felt I deserved to be sad, which is wrong.

Stage 4: Depression, Loneliness and Reflection

Elizabeth Kübler-Ross said, "Depression may feel like a 'quiet' stage of grief. In the early stages of loss, you may be running from the emotions, trying to stay a step ahead of them. By this point, however, you may be able to embrace and work through them more healthfully." I chose to isolate myself from others to reflect and cope with the loss entirely. However, the isolation led to a messy depression.

I couldn't fully define the depression I felt a couple of months after the loss, but I didn't know how to go forward. Several times, I felt worse than the first few weeks of the loss. However, having the tenacity to be there for my kids pushed me to seek help. My loved ones' prayers and attending the grief share program at Springs Church slowly started to help me.

Grieving can feel overwhelming; we may feel foggy, heavy, and confused. Depression may feel like the unavoidable landing point of any loss. However, if we feel stuck there or can't seem to move past this stage of grief, it is better to talk with a mental health expert. A therapist can help us work through this period of coping.

Stage 5: Acceptance

Grief is very personal, and we may feel something different every time. We may need several weeks, or grief may be years long. I have started to put pieces of my life back together and move forward. However, I still struggle to accept such an energetic, loving, caring, and passionate man was gone. I sometimes still shed some tears, and I know this new way of life is a very gradual journey.

Acceptance doesn't mean we've moved past the grief or loss. However, it does mean that we've accepted the loss and understand what it means in our life now. There's been a significant change in our lives, which upends the way we think about many things. Elizabeth Kübler-Ross said, "Look to acceptance as a way to see that there may be more good days than bad, but there may still be bad—and that's OK."

The key to understanding grief is realizing that no one experiences the same thing. During grief, people may encourage us to "be strong" or "not to cry." But how sad it would be if someone we cared about died and we didn't cry, or we carried on as if nothing had happened. I agree with Dr. Bill Webster, who said, "I'd like to think that someone will miss me enough to shed a tear after I'm gone. Wouldn't you? Admittedly, saying that grief is NORMAL does not minimize its DIFFICULTY. It may be one of the most challenging experiences of our life."

Grieving is a very personal matter, and we shouldn't expect people to understand our feelings fully. "Each heart knows its own bitterness" (Proverbs 14:10 , NIV). Our loss seems like the worst possible thing that could have happened to us. I recently facilitated a grief share discussion with my community, and someone asked if it is more difficult to lose a child than a spouse. We have also discussed if it is worse to lose someone unexpectedly in an accident or after a long illness. While each loss is different, experts say the worst kind of loss is yours. When you lose a significant person from your life, whatever the relationship, it's sad, it hurts, and nothing takes away from your right to feel the loss and grief of the absence of that person from your life.

Loss is difficult, and grief is painful. However, the only way out of it is to go through it. Understanding the grief process has no shortcut, and finding the courage to go through it plays a major key to recovery. Our process is special and unique depending on what has been lost from our life. It takes a toll on us emotionally and physically. It requires hard work and God's grace.

The process of grief may take a long time. Particularly, the first year was very intense for me. Three years later, I sometimes find myself in the depths of despair. I cannot predict the sad feelings. It can be triggered anytime, so I had to meditate on encouraging words continually. Grief comes and goes and takes much longer than most people expect. Most people may be expecting us to get over it quickly because they don't understand what is normal in grief. However, we should walk through it at our pace. Finding a community group, such as grief share, where others who have been through the deep places share their experiences, can be a real help. Dr. Bill Webster said, "Grief is about coping with the loss of a relationship, and often in a supporting relationship, healing can be found." For me, my active relationship with God through meditating His word, my beloved friends, and my church community are helping me enormously.

11
THINGS NOT TO DO/ SAY TO A GRIEVING PERSON

When we try to help someone who's grieving, it's essential to understand the facts about grief and the process of grieving mentioned in the previous chapter. Grieving is a personal experience, and there's no right or wrong way. How a person grieves depends on many factors, including personality and coping style, life experience, and faith, to name a few. The process of grieving takes time; healing happens gradually—it can't be forced or rushed. Some people start to feel better in months; for others, it may take years, and some may grieve forever. If you support a grieving person, it's crucial to be patient and allow the process to unfold naturally. The pain of grief may never fully heal. Be sensitive to the fact that life may never feel the same.

I have gathered the following realities from my own experiences and others to help you understand what some of the things we say and do are not helpful to a grieving person. This is from our personal grieving point of view, and I acknowledge you may disagree with some of the suggestions.

1. Let's avoid saying anything to diminish it. Perhaps the death is related to an ex rather than a current partner? It doesn't matter. If they're sad, they're sad.

2. We shouldn't cross the street to avoid talking to them. I've noticed a person whom I knew backing away from me to avoid a chat. My friend shared the same experience with me while grieving the loss of her mother. My friend passionately said, "I would like to shout at those people who are running away from us; it is annoying! What we're going through isn't contagious—but what you're doing is estranging, insensitive, hurtful, and rude." My other friend argued, "The reason we avoid you is because we get overwhelmed and don't know what to say, hence to avoid a very awkward situation." I understand his point; however, it's helpful to acknowledge your avoidance hurts the grieving person more.

3. I suggest not to compare it to your experience unless it's a fitting comparison. It's such instinct, but if your great-grandpa died in his 90s while asleep, as opposed to an accidental death of a young person, I'm just not going to want to hear comparing it. The extreme example I heard was when a woman's only child died by suicide at age thirty, and a friend wrote to her, "I know exactly how you feel because my dog just died."

4. Don't only focus on the good. Finding positives can be great but don't polish the situation. Similarly, don't put a positive spin on everything they're saying.

5. It's not helpful to comment on their appearance. This may put pressure on the person to keep up appearances. You may think it looks like they're doing well, smiling and laughing at church over the weekend. But unless you check on them at 3:00 a.m. when they're alone in the dark, crying on their pillow about the pain of grief, you don't have any idea. What we all do know, though, is that appearances can be deceiving. And if there are physical indicators they're suffering, don't comment on that either. I lost a lot of hair for a while, and whatever remained turned into grey. Even though I understood his well-meant intentions, I didn't appreciate the criticism I received from a friend who asked me, "Why are you neglecting yourself?"

6. It's better not to say, "I know how you feel." Though you may have experienced a loss, it's an overwhelmingly personal experience. You're never truly able to know how someone experiences the loss and claiming that you know it can feel invalidating.

7. Some people say, "We are all going to die; it will happen to all of us eventually." Obviously, everyone experiences death and loss as a part of life, but this perspective might minimize the actual loss at the moment.

8. I would suggest not to say, "You're so strong. You're handling this better than I expected." This may create mixed feelings in the grieving person. It puts pressure on the person to hide their true feelings.

9. Some religious people say, "They're in a better place" when the person is during the first phases of grieving.

This phrase can de-emphasize the pain we're feeling at the moment. What's challenging about the loss is the person is gone, and we're suffering the loss alone. The message from Pastor Leon on Heaven gave me hope when I was in the "acceptance" phase of the grieving process. However, I wouldn't have been as receptive to it if I heard it when I was in the "angry" stage. Discern the situation.

10. We shouldn't push a grieving person to move on. Many people don't understand "moving on" is not something we wanted to do. Together, we had created too much to simply leave. The idea of moving on and leaving the life we created together behind doesn't feel right. Even though staying stuck isn't what grievers want, I found the comments to "move on" very irritating.

11. I suggest not to say, "Let me know if there's anything I can do for you." It sounds helpful, but it puts the responsibility on the grieving person to reach out for help. If that person is very independent and not comfortable asking for help, this becomes a void promise. We're all busy, but if you want to help a grieving person, don't wait. Just do it.

12. I found it not helpful to ask, "How are you doing?" We are all used to this well-worn phrase in our day to day greetings; however, for a grieving person, it adds pressure because it's obvious we're not doing well, but it's very uncomfortable to admit that. So, we respond with "fine" or "ok." This question doesn't allow us to communicate our feelings.

13. I suggest not to say, "You can always get remarried or have another child." You might be thinking you're helping them to see hope. However, to the bereaved, it sounds like you're diminishing the importance of

the person who died and suggesting a loved one is replaceable.

14. Don't say, "I didn't call because I thought you wanted to be alone." Even if the person grieving told you he or she wanted to be alone, you should always call, write, email, or text. If you really care, you would anyway.

15. I didn't like it when some people asked me, "Did the kids ask you about their dad?" or "Do they remember him?" Unfortunately, I was asked this question multiple times, and my answer was, of course, they will remember him for the rest of their life. I guess the awkwardness of death can cause some people to forget common sense.

12
HOW CAN WE HELP?

Knowing the right way of helping and the right things to say to a grieving person don't come naturally. People generally avoid talking about death and grieving. Many people haven't had much experience with people in desperate emotional pain. It's not always obvious how we can help a grieving person—we're neither born with that skill nor taught. Even after we have gone through the pain ourselves, our experience may not be the same as others because every grieving person is unique. There's no ultimate solution to a grieving person; however, the following guidance could lessen the pain. Again, this isn't a holistic list; they are some supporting ideas based on my personal experience and what I agreed with others who shared theirs.

1. It is good to acknowledge just how painful it really is. You can say, "I can only imagine how you're feeling." This gives the person a chance to identify how

he or she feels, rather than speaking for him or her. Acknowledge what the person is going through at the moment is very painful. Don't expect grieving people to polish over their feelings; let them grieve fully and without judgment. You can also say, "It's really tough right now for you."

I personally found comfort in others, agreeing that things were horrible, and they can only imagine the magnitude of the pain. This will usually be more supportive than telling someone that it's not that bad or "could be worse."

2. Express your care/love creatively. I've had friends force themselves into my house even though I've said I'm fine because they knew it wasn't true. Aida and Abush are an exemplary couple in our GFMM church who I love dearly. After everyone left to their day to day life, one Saturday in particular, they dedicated the entire day to spend quality time with the kids and me. Even though, I was not ready for visitors, I sensed their companionship that specific day helped me combat my depression and lifted our spirit. I have also appreciated the postcards, formal bereavement letters, obituary notes, voice messages, emails, WhatsApp texts, Viber and Facebook messages, and handmade postcards from Isaiah's AWANA kids. If there was any good intention there, whatever it was, I appreciated it. Even if it only helped slightly, that was something, and I still go back and reread some of them. Being sad is lonely. I have appreciated the regular note I have received from my friends, even though sometimes it only says, "Thinking of you and praying for you."

3. I encourage you to listen. If the grieving person initiates a conversation, make space for their words

without necessarily feeling the need to interject. We have such problem-solving attitudes in our society, but it's unlikely you can fix this situation. Without any magical thing to say to make it all better, just give them the space to express themselves and feel heard. I don't usually talk about how I feel. However, I'm blessed with many good friends who would've listened for hours if I need them to. I have also learned to put every effort into being a good listener to my friends and clients who need my attention.

4. Discern their reaction. Everyone grieves differently and may get supported differently. We need to pay attention to their response. Last winter, I visited grieving parents who lost their firstborn. The family was new to Canada, and their son was tragically killed a few weeks before they arrived. I felt the family needed some emotional help and offered my listening ears, but I realized they didn't like discussing their son's loss. I quickly backed off and changed the subject. If you've said something kind, and they don't want to hear more than that, be sensitive and change the subject to make it easier for them.

5. You can say, "I wish I had the right words for you." A grieving person may not appreciate people who say whatever comes to their mouth or the people who just keep silent. It's better to find a balance. I've experienced both in my personal journey, and I didn't know what to say to stop the chatters or break the silence. I assure you, it wasn't comfortable.

6. It's ok to say, "I'm sorry you're suffering." If the person who died suffered from a long-time illness, the person could be glad their loved one is not suffering anymore, but it doesn't make the pain of grieving less;

we need to focus on the person suffering the pain at the moment.

7. You can say, "You must really miss them." The loss of a loved one is likely the source of the pain—focus on that, rather than brushing it aside as a non-negotiable aspect of life.

8. Just reach out. You might feel the urge to hold back out of fear that you'll remind them of the bad news again, but it's probably always inescapably in their minds. So, just say something. The feeling that someone cares about you and your pain can be so comforting. I had people I barely knew express genuine sympathy, and it helped.

9. Move forward. I paid attention to this word during the grief share session at Springs Church. It really helped me focus on the next small step I needed to take to get through the heavy days. Even now, it keeps reminding me to consider what I needed to let go of that no longer helps me and focus on my next step.

10. Offering concrete suggestions help. "I'll come over to clean the house and do a few loads of laundry on Saturday," or "I'll take the kids to the school bus for the next month." Specific offers are more comfortable to accept than a wide-open request. Make the food; tell them when you're coming around to cut the lawn; offer to pick their children up from school that day. Just do it.

11. You can say, "You might not be feeling great, but that's ok." Let the grieving people have complete freedom to feel how they feel without having the burden of being judged by others. They may need to be vulnerable and cry, or they may be singing and laughing. Let them

feel whatever they are feeling, and whenever they are feeling is ok.

12. I would like to honor him/her this way. Tie your memorials to your existing knowledge base. Tap into your memories and information about the person and acknowledge that it symbolizes your two shared relationships.

13. Share memories. One of the most helpful things you can do for a grieving person is to share a memory of their loved one. You can also help them focus on the memories by asking specific questions and being active listeners. My friend Debo was great at telling me stories she gathered from people telling her how Isaiah's kindness had touched them. I still appreciate it when people share beautiful memories because he will never get a chance to make a new story.

14. In my culture, they say, "ጽንዓት ይሃብካ" for male and "ጽንዓት ይሃብኪ." for female. These two words are very powerful, and the closest translation I can make is "May God give you the grace, resilience, and endurance to remain strong." I like this word as it acknowledges you may not be able to overcome grief alone but can with God's divine power and strength. I encourage the Tigrigna speaking community to use it if they don't know what to say to a grieving person.

15. A simple and heartfelt expression may be just enough and most needed or useful. I found a kind hug with "I am so sorry for your loss" was the simplest and the best.

16. If you are a person of faith, and the grieving person gives you permission, please pray for them and with them. For several months after the loss, I had

lost confidence in prayer, and if it was not for my friend who persistently prayed with me, I might have remained in a messy depression for a very long time.

13
SUPPORTING A
GRIEVING CHILD

When I was about ten years old, a horrible thing happened to our family. My dad's youngest brother was brutally executed by the Ethiopian regime for no reason. I remember how my parents were devastated by the sad news, especially my mom, who was weeping every morning for months. I remember my uncle was a very loving person, and he had brought us some fresh corn, beans, and fresh vegetables from his garden when he came to our city to distribute his produce. He was loved by the young and adults for his generosity and loving heart. We had lost our grandpa and other family members before then; however, I remember this specific loss was extremely painful to our family. It was a brutal murder that no one expected.

According to our custom, different people came to pay respect early in the morning, around 6:00 a.m., while we were sleeping. The women would chant while weeping. I'm not sure if the visitors were equally impacted, but I knew my mom was shedding a lot of tears to the extent that it was sometimes challenging for her to see. I started to fear that my mom would become blind or die from sorrow. I hated the visitors because all they did from my perspective was made my mom weep; my heart kept sinking whenever I saw my mom crying. It was tough for me to process what was going on. There was no one paying attention to the horrible emotions we were experiencing as kids. I wish the tradition was a bit more sensitive to kids.

In my current grief, I heard the tragic news around 10:00 p.m. My personality is one that when I get shocked, I become dead silent. I couldn't say anything, and our church family stayed overnight with me. So, the first thing I did was take my kids to my brother's house because I didn't want them to see the cultural mourning practices; thankfully, my brother lives across the street. Then, I calmly told the horrible news to them myself. Not only my kids but my nephews and nieces were also very close to Isaiah, so they were devastated by the horrific news. Some of them cried; some of them were very quiet. I allowed them to ask questions and tried to answer them as age-appropriately as possible. Since Isaiah and I knew a lot of people, I had guests almost every day for three weeks. So, the kids stayed at my brother's house while I checked on them daily. I took them to the funeral with me and allowed them to say goodbye to the body. Both my son and daughter got sick to their stomach after the funeral; they couldn't handle the stress, and it was tough for us. However, I spent some more time with them after the funeral, and despite my sorrow, I tried my best to assure them that God was with us and we would be fine.

After the funeral, we started our new normal. Thank God I could take a leave from work, which helped me be able to monitor the kids closely and make sure they were supported. I offered to take them to a counseling service, but they said they didn't need it. So, I had to wear my coaching hat and tried to walk them through the process. I've noticed children grieve differently. All my kids were very close to their dad, but their response to the situation varied. One of my daughters didn't show any external impression; however, she started wetting her bed. She wouldn't eat, and she would cry about any silly thing.

In contrast, my other two kids would ask questions and try to understand the situation. The main thing that helped them move forward was extracurricular activities. My son loved basketball, so I signed him up for a basketball team. My older daughter was into gymnastics. To be honest, I didn't like driving across the city to different tournaments; however, they never missed any class, and it helped distract them from the pain of the loss. I know they still grieve the loss at different times, so I pay attention, pray for them, and provide support as much as I can.

Faith, my middle child, loves cooking, just like her dad. On the eve of last Father's Day, she asked me if she could cook breakfast for her brother, Joseph, on behalf of Isaiah. I felt sad; I knew she missed her dad, but I pretended to take it lightly and said, "No problem at all. Let's ask Joseph." Unfortunately, he didn't like the idea at all, so I suggested to Faith that we cook together for everyone. So, on Father's Day morning, we cooked Isaiah's favourite breakfast, and I allowed her to vent while busy cooking. However, we were very quiet while eating. I could see on my children's faces how much they missed their dad. I felt a bit awkward discussing the topic but decided to confront the situation and help them open up. I started by opening a discussion about Father's Day and explained that our earthly fathers also enjoy God's fatherhood. So, our ultimate father is God, and He promised us He won't leave us fatherless. (John 14:18 , NIV). Faith requested that we listen to a Father's Day song sung by her friend from Springs Church. We listened to that song several times.

It was a very tough morning, and I thought I handled it well; however, I thanked God I finished breakfast without having to run away to the washroom to cry. After breakfast with the kids, I took a walk to release the pressure. When I was coming back from my walk, I met a couple of the fathers in my neighborhood, chatting while one of them was holding a lawnmower, which looked like mine. I said hello and stopped to ask them some questions about the lawnmower because mine wasn't working. They gave me some tips, and one of them kindly said, "Let me know if it doesn't work. I'll come to check it out for you later." Suddenly in the middle of the conversation, my eyes filled with tears. I did my best to gather myself. I wished them a happy Father's Day. After walking away as fast as I could, I started sobbing like crazy. I decided to go back to the beautiful park in the neighborhood, sat down on a bench, and cried as much as I wanted. I think I needed to release the pressure that was building in my chest. Sometimes, it's hard to imagine how the kids would feel on certain occasions. They seemed to do well on the previous two Father's Days, but it seemed this one triggered a bit of emotion in all of us. I can't be a father to my children. However, I know God is our everlasting Father, and I pray for God's grace to equip them to move forward.

Helping the kids is a long-time commitment. We have a culture of planning as a family. Every Sunday, we roughly plan for the week ahead, and every evening after supper, we check on what the plan will be for the next day. That helps me make sure they have the correct number of items on their plate to support their mental focus. However, there have been moments when we've broken down, wept as a family, and reread the hundreds of notes we have received from Isaiah's Bible students and other family and friends. Their friends' parents also played a significant role in my children's grieving and healing process by taking them for a play date and driving them to Bible study and church. We're very involved in our

community, and thanks to God, there's always someone who reaches out to help. After all, it takes a village to raise a kid.

Part 4 — Let Us Reflect

1. Do you understand God's grace?

2. Do you know anyone who is grieving any kind of loss?

3. How are you planning to support that person?

4. Do you know any child who is grieving a loss?

5. What can you do to support the child?

PART 5
GOD'S GRACE AND MERCY

One drop of the Lord's mercy is better than an ocean of the world's comfort.

—Lysa Terkeurst

14
LEAN ON GOD'S GRACE

I'm not new to grief. I was born and raised in Eritrea during a war and lost several precious cousins, uncles, and friends to different casualties. Even after I left my home country and came to the world's relatively peaceful zone, I've faced several heartaches. However, I have been prevailing against several unpleasant circumstances by letting go of my self-reliance and depending entirely on God's grace for strength. Leaning on God doesn't happen like magic, but you grow in it as you trust what the Bible reveals about His character and promises. God gives strength to the weary and increases the power of the weak (Isaiah 40:29-31,NIV). I started a close relationship with God about twenty-three years ago, and I've never regretted that choice. I've suffered several losses in those years, including my parents and husband; things often felt terrible in my life. However, I am determined to be a parasite of God. Yes, I am

100% dependent on God, and I know for sure He is in and with me. There were times when it didn't feel like He was with me. In hindsight, God was there for me every step of the way.

Losing a loved one isn't the only source of sorrow. Even elusive losses in life can trigger a sense of grief. You might grieve after moving away from home, breaking up with friends, changing jobs, or changing neighborhoods, to name a few. Whatever your loss, it's personal to you. You shouldn't feel ashamed about how you feel or believe it's somehow only appropriate to grieve for some issues. If the person, pet, relationship, or situation was significant to you, it's normal to suffer because of the loss you're experiencing. Whatever the cause of your grief and the magnitude of the pain, there are healthy ways to cope and eventually move forward with your life. That coping mechanism for me was leaning on the grace of God. Many people think talking about God's grace is a non-tangible cliché, and I don't blame them. It's a hidden treasure that you can only take advantage of by surrendering to the guidance of the Holy Spirit and holy scriptures. Our nature is more inclined to do rather than rest and yield, so the fight is to quiet our soul to get the full advantage of resting in God and leaning on His grace.

Grace is beyond our limited understanding. The Merriam Webster dictionary defined grace as "a virtue coming from God." Grace in Christianity is the free and unmerited favor of God as manifested in sinners' salvation and the bestowing of blessings. For me, grace is a divine capacity—a gift from God that enables us to live our daily life and overcome or endure any difficult situations, including grief. Since what I want to emphasize in this book is God's grace, I have dug a bit to explore the understanding of grace, and I have listed its scriptural usage below:

In the New Testament, the word translated as grace is the Greek word, Charis (/ˈkeɪrɪs/; Ancient Greek: χάρις), for which Strong's Concordance gives this definition: "Graciousness (as gratifying), of manner or act (abstract or concrete; literal, figurative or spiritual; especially the divine influence upon the heart, and its reflection in the life; including gratitude)."Grieving is personal disappointment at its maximum level, and based on my personal experience, I learned God's grace could walk us through its process and help us see beyond the hurt. Grieving can press you down until you become so devastated that you lose a desire to live; however, grace could lift you against the pressure of the darkness if you allow it. The grieving process can go on for a very long time; I think some of the losses are never possible to get over by our might. However, if we're wise and have the support and courage to deal with it, the loss will begin to lose its controlling power. Grieving can control our lives and destroy them forever if we're not careful. However, we can intentionally deal with it wisely.

I had to either allow the loss to continue to destroy me or choose to lean on God's grace to help me adjust and overcome. Overall, life is a choice, so I made my choice as a believer to not allow the darkness of loss to overpower me. I said to myself, *I have to do whatever it takes to make the loss lose its controlling power over me.* I started by acknowledging that behind the untimely loss was the devil, not God, and believed that God was for me, God was with me, and His grace would enable me to overcome the darkness of grieving. God says, "...I will not in any way fail you nor give you up nor leave you without support... [I will] not in any degree leave you helpless nor forsake nor let [you] down..." (Hebrews 13:5, AMP). I started by focusing on God and meditating on His promises for me. I understood God is ready, willing, and able to pick me up.

15
OUR PERCEPTION OF GOD VS. HIS GRACE

It is the nature of grace always to fill spaces that have been empty.

—Goethe

Please allow me to walk you a bit further regarding grace. After humans separate from God, mankind perceives God and His gifts in a corrupted way. For example, let's examine how the Israelites, who were supposed to be God's chosen people in the old testament, perceived God in the following scripture:

With what shall I come before the Lord and bow down before the exalted God? Shall I come before him with burnt offerings, with calves a year old? Will the Lord be pleased with thousands of rams, with ten thousand rivers of olive oil? Shall I offer my firstborn for my transgression, the fruit of my body for the sin of my soul? He has shown you, O mortal, what is good. And what does the Lord require of you? To act justly and to love mercy and to walk humbly with your God. (Micah 6:6-8, NIV)

If we read Micah's entire book, chapters one through five, God reminded them about the great miracles He had done and how He rescued them from the Egyptians; He was rebuking them with love. In chapter six, their response sounds impressive—they were concerned about what to bring to God. However, God wasn't worried about what they brought Him, but who they needed to be. Intentionally or unintentionally, the people in this chapter put God's picture as a cruel authority figure who wasn't easy to please and expected something from them. God is perfect in His ways; He begins in love and finishes in love. Even when he reprimands, He does it in love.

Grace is a perfect gift from God, and it reflects the character of the giver, not the receiver's identity. It begins at the cross, and it's beyond our knowledge and understanding.

"Out of his fullness, we have all received grace in place ofgrace already given" (John 1:16-17, NIV).

God is beyond a generous giver, and His first gift is His precious son, Jesus Christ. No matter how much we love each other, we wouldn't dare to give any one of our children as a sacrifice on behalf of one another. However, God loved us so muchthat He gave us His only son.

"For God so loved the world that he gave his one and only Son, that whoever believes in him shall not perish but have eternal life" (John 3:16, NIV).

You may have heard this verse before, and it may sound easy, but it's the foundation of our salvation. God gave His only son, so the world wouldn't perish. This verse speaks volumes about the grace of God and shows the special love God has for humanity.

> "For the grace of God has appeared that offers salvation to all people" (Titus 2:11, NIV).

We receive grace not because we deserve it but through God's generosity and mercy and unmerited favour. Grace is related to faith. God has accomplished salvation by grace, and it doesn't require your contribution to be saved aside from a willingness to receive the divine gift. Grace was given to us before we were conceived, and we receive the gift of grace by believing in Christ Jesus. God has already provided the grace, and we can accept it by faith.

> But because of his great love for us, God, who is rich in mercy, made us alive with Christ even when we were dead in transgressions—it is by grace you have been saved. And God raised us up with Christ and seated us with him in the heavenly realms in Christ Jesus, in order that in the coming ages he might show the incomparable riches of his grace, expressed in his kindness to us in Christ Jesus. For it is by grace you have been saved, through faith—and this is not from yourselves, it is the gift of God. (Eph 2:4-8, NIV)

Grace has saved us; however, it's not because of who we are; it's simply God's generous gift. It's not related to our works and deeds.

> "Now to the one who works, wages are not credited as a gift but as an obligation. However, to the one who does not work but trusts God who justifies the ungodly, their faith is credited as righteousness" (Rom 4:4-5, NIV).

The expectation from us is to believe and receive God's grace and accept Christ as our savior.

"Let us then approach God's throne of grace with confidence, so that we may receive mercy and find grace to help us in our time of need" (Heb 4:16 , NIV).

We understand the grace of God based on the picture we have about God Himself. Our knowledge about God determines our understanding of grace. Therefore, we need to start with God. Primarily, we need to know God.

"The Lord appeared to us in the past, saying: I have loved you with an everlasting love; I have drawn you with unfailing kindness" (Jer 31:3, NIV).

God is the same in the past, in the present, and in the future. God is Spirit and Love, and it doesn't change through time. His love is in spirit, and it doesn't change with our attitude or actions. God always loves us; even when He reprimands, He starts and ends in love.

We don't have the potential to describe the grace of God. In the following passage, the Bible referred to it as an indescribable gift.

"And in their prayers for you, their hearts will go out to you, because of the surpassing grace God has given you. Thanks be to God for his indescribable gift!" (2 Cor 9:14-15, NIV).

Grace is a gift that shouldn't be taken lightly. I've added some more verses on the amazing grace of God below. I encourage you to take some time and ponder on them:

I became a servant of this gospel by the gift of God's grace given me through the working of his power. Although I am less than the least of all the Lord's people, this grace was given me: to preach to the Gentiles the boundless riches of Christ, and to make plain to everyone the administration of this mystery, which for ages past was kept hidden in God, who created all things. (Eph 3:7-9, NIV)

"What shall we say, then? Shall we go on sinning so that grace may increase? By no means! We are those who have died to sin; how can we live in it any longer?" (Rom 6:1-2, NIV)

"For certain individuals whose condemnation was written about long ago have secretly slipped in among you. They are ungodly people, who pervert the grace of our God into a license for immorality and deny Jesus Christ our only Sovereign and Lord" (Jude 1:4, NIV).

He has saved us and called us to a holy life—not because of anything we have done but because of his own purpose and grace. This grace was given us in Christ Jesus before the beginning of time, but it has now been revealed through the appearing of our Savior, Christ Jesus, who has destroyed death and has brought life and immortality to light through the gospel. (2 Tim 1:9-10, NIV)

But he said to me, "My grace is sufficient for you, for my power is made perfect in weakness." Therefore, I will boast all the more gladly about my weaknesses, so that Christ's power may rest on me. That is why, for Christ's sake, I delight in weaknesses, in insults, in hardships, in persecutions, in difficulties. For when I am weak, then I am strong. (2 Cor 12:9-10, NIV)

In summary, grace is a perfect gift from our Creator that shouldn't be taken lightly. Whoever you are—rich or poor, tall or short, black or white—I encourage you to know God through His word and be strong in the grace that is in Christ Jesus.

"Now I commit you to God and to the word of his grace, which can build you up and give you an inheritance among all those who are sanctified" (Acts 20:32, NIV).

16
WHAT'S NEXT?

My main desire for the reader of this book is to move forward and have you one step closer to God. If you know God already and have a spiritual relationship with him, I would like to encourage you to get closer to Him and live your purpose by taking advantage of His grace. Perhaps you are grieving a loss; please don't allow the loss to get in between you and what you're designed to do. If you are new to the concept of knowing God, my prayers are for your spiritual eyes to open so that you can understand the physical world is governed by the spiritual world and lean on God's grace to obtain the correct spiritual revelation that's crucial to your life. The pain of grief can often cause you to want to withdraw from God or others and retreat into your closet. However, communing with God and having the support of other people is vital to healing from loss. Even if you're not comfortable talking about your emotional state under normal circumstances, it's important to express them when you're grieving.

Sharing your loss with others can make the burden of grief easier to carry; however, that doesn't mean you need to talk about your loss every time you interact with friends and family. Your grief can be confusing, especially if they haven't experienced a similar loss themselves. Many people feel awkward when trying to comfort someone who's grieving. They may feel unsure about how to comfort you and end up saying or doing the wrong things. But don't use that as an excuse to retreat and avoid social contact. If a friend or loved one reaches out to you, it's because they care, and comfort can come from just being around others who care about you.

My youngest sister enabled me by taking care of my kids while I went to a women's retreat on my birthday weekend a few months after my loss. Learning how to ride a horse during that vacation helped my mind experience something different and helped me make some new long-lasting friends. Don't isolate yourself; turn to friends and family members. Now is the time to lean on the people who care about you, even if you take pride in being strong and self-sufficient. Rather than avoiding them, draw friends and loved ones close, spend time together, and don't be shy to accept the assistance offered. Often, people want to help but don't know how, so tell them what you need—whether it's a shoulder to cry on, help with the kids, cooking, cleaning, or just someone to hang out with. If you don't feel you have anyone you can regularly connect with in person, it's never too late to build new friendships. Our pastor says if you want friends, be friendly. Sometimes we want people to recognize our pain and be nice to us; however, we never know what they are going through either, so it is ok to take the initiative to be friendly and make some new friends. In fact, sometimes it gives you a fresh breath to hang around new friends who don't know about your loss. I have lots of precious friends who are irreplaceable, but I continue to add new ones into my circle by God's grace.

There are still times when I struggle to get out of my shell with people, but I press on, releasing the pressure in prayers to God. At times, it was very difficult for me to flow in prayers until I listened to some good preachers. (Mainly, I listened to Pastor Leon Fontaine or Pastor Chris Oyakhilome.) I also didn't give in to my feelings; sometimes, after I pushed myself to do it consistently, my spirit slowly started to take off. Repeating the words of the "Rhapsody of Realities" devotional articles played a vital role in getting me back into spiritual shape. Perhaps, you have very little time to hang out with people. God is there any time and anywhere, so keep talking to Him; He is the very present help. Take some time to dig more into His word, listen to good preachers, meditate, and focus on what you can do. Trust me; nothing will fill the gap in life the way God does. You won't get the true meaning of life until you've built the relationship with the author of life. You may achieve fame and material success, but if your inner person is not satisfied by connecting to the ultimate source, all your hard work will feel in vain. Death is a supreme teacher to understand the correct perspective on life if we allow it.

Above all, we can draw comfort from our faith in God and lean into His grace. One of the names of the Holy Spirit is "Paraclete," which means a helper. God is referred to in the Bible as a comforter: "Praise be to the God and Father of our Lord Jesus Christ, the Father of compassion and the God of all comfort, who comforts us in all our troubles, so that we can comfort those in any trouble with the comfort we ourselves receive from God" (2 Corinthians 1:3-4, NIV). Embrace the comfort God can provide. Even when you don't feel it start, continuing Spiritual activities that are meaningful to you—such as praying, meditating, or going to church— can offer consolation. I questioned my faith in the wake of the loss. However, listening to good preachers and joining a grief share group in our church helped me regain my spiritual strength. Grief can feel very lonely, even when you have loved ones around. Sharing my sorrow with others who experienced similar losses was helpful to me. To find a bereavement support group in your area, contact local hospitals, hospices, funeral homes, and counseling centers, or see the coaching service provided at the end of this book.

For people in the west, we are blessed with many resources around us, and we have access to professional grief counselors. My interaction with one of the top qualified grief counselors was helpful to some extent. He gave me some great tools and techniques to navigate through the intense emotions and overcome some obstacles. However, I found more meaningful help by talking to people who passed through similar losses. Fortunately, I was a member of the Igniting Souls Tribe, and I had access to several members who are warriors and survived horrific losses. In the tribe, there are several authors and life coaches. Honestly speaking, I may not have written this book had I not associated with them. For example, reading a book written by a mother who lost four kids within a few years and listening to her inspiring messages has been a source of strength and wisdom for me.

I have also decided to pay it forward and build a community of support to share our feelings and care for each other. Support groups and communities play a vital role in healing broken hearts. Additionally, I'm building a mindset session tailored to help grieving people as part of my life coaching program. As a person who knows grief from a challenging, personal experience, I desire to give some hope to the hurting world. My prayers are the sessions will provide you with some tools to work through the intense emotions of grieving and move forward at your own pace.

There's life beyond the loss; it's time to reinvent; it is time to experience a new beginning. I didn't understand these before, but I have learned several lessons from my horrible loss.

1. Death taught me I should never take those I love for granted.

2. Death made me aware of my mortality and helped me to savor what's happening now.

3. Death vests the present with meaning.

4. Death helped me remember the countless blessings in my life—at this very moment.

5. Death taught me life is short, and there's no point worrying your way through it.

Let me close this chapter with the advice I received from one of my dearest beloved friends, Dawit Tesfamicael. He said in Tigrigna, "ጓሞት ሕኔለ፥ ከለኸ ሰሓቕ እያ።." I found there are many hidden treasures in my ethnic culture that aren't easy to translate into English. This saying is one of them. The closest interpretation I can give for this one is, "We can either laugh in the face of death or die trying not to." There's nothing we can do to bring our loved ones back; however, we can continue their legacy by serving others and taking care of ourselves. It seems selfish to some and unattainable to others, but through God's grace, it's possible. Let's continue to lean on God's grace.

17
EMBRACE HIS CALL

At a Christmas party, I asked a dear friend, who's a very successful businessman, if he believed in God or His son, Jesus Christ. He said, "Why do I need God?" and added, "God is only for poor people. I don't need to bother God for anything; he has a suffering world that needs him."

In a way, his answer indicated he believed in a God who can take care of the poor and the needy. So, I acknowledged his understanding, and I asked him, "Do you know what the Bible advises to rich people?"

He was curious. "No, I've never read the Bible. What does it say?"

I told him the Bible says, "Charge them that are rich in this world, that they be not high-minded, nor trust in uncertain riches, but in the living God, who giveth us richly all things to enjoy" (1 Timothy 6:17, NIV). Then, I continued, "I know you're financially stable, you're a hard worker, and you have a beautiful family, but are you enjoying your life?"

He said, "It depends. I enjoy it sometimes, and I hate the stress of life at other times, and with the current ups and downs of the economy, I can't sleep at peace most nights."

I acknowledged his reality and shared a bit about God's relevance to our day-to-day lives. Then, I referred him to listen to Pastor Leon Fountain's messages on YouTube.

God's love is without limits; God is gracious and kind to all, no matter who they are. His love for man is beyond human comprehension. John 15:13 (KJV) says, "Greater love hath no man than this, that a man lay down his life for his friends." God took on an image of a man and came to Earth to show us the way. The Lord Jesus laid down His life for us like no one ever did. He was divine and without sin; yet, He became the sin-sacrifice, offered up for the sin of the world. He was crucified of His own will in the place of others. Think about it: He took the place of our sin on the cross so that we might take His place of righteousness. "For he hath made him be sin for us, who knew no sin; that we might be made the righteousness of God in him" (2 Corinthians 5:21, KJV). How do you describe such love that made Him die for sinners—the criminals, murderers, robbers, etc.? He came, lived, worked wonders, died, and was resurrected all for the love of mankind. Everything He did was for the love of mankind. He declared His purpose for coming in John 10:10 ; it was so we could have life and live it fully. The life He's given us is one of blessings, joy, and pleasures forevermore. The joy and pleasure we attain through Christ are undiminished by the challenges we face.

There have been more than enough religions globally, and I am convinced that Jesus Christ didn't come to build another religion; He came to give us life. He came to pay the price for our sanctification and to show us the way; He is the way, the truth, and the life. All we need is to have faith in Him and trust in His finished works. "For by grace are ye saved through faith; and that not of yourselves: it is the gift of God: Not of works, lest any man should boast" (Ephesians 2:8-9, KJV).

Some think they ought to be accepted by God or blessed by Him for their good works; they believe in their self-righteousness. But what God rewards is your faith in the finished works of Christ, His substitutionary work on your behalf. The Apostle Paul revealed the fruitlessness of trusting in your good works or observance of His law to answer for you before God. He wrote,

> ...I count all things but loss for the excellency of the knowledge of Christ Jesus my Lord: for whom I have suffered the loss of all things, and do count them but dung, that I may win Christ, And be found in him, not having my own righteousness, which is of the law, but that which is through the faith of Christ, the righteousness which is of God by faith. (Philippians 3:8-9, NIV)

The key concept is to be found in Christ, not to have your own righteousness. Accept God's righteousness through the faith of Christ Jesus. Never try to impress God with your "religiosity;" He has already blessed you with ALL the spiritual blessings in heavenly places in Christ (Ephesians 1:3, NIV). There's nothing you could ever want that isn't already yours in Christ. Everything He owns belongs to you.

I believe we can have and enjoy our best life now, and God is fine with it. Life is a gift and a calling from God. Everything in life, including the world around us, was created for our benefit. All we need to enjoy life to the fullest is to be ourselves and stay in God's Word. Jesus said, "...I came that they may have and enjoy life, and have it in abundance (to the full, till it overflows)" (John 10:10 [Amplified Bible Classic Edition]). Think about that! Enjoying our life is a choice we have to make for ourselves if we want to have God's best today and for all time. We also read God has given you richly (not sparsely) ALL things to ENJOY. What we need is to spend time with the Word, to know what's ours in Christ Jesus, so we can live by His Word and enjoy our life to the fullest, for His glory. We're not immune from suffering; however, having God on our side makes a lot of difference during the process.

Finally, I would like to encourage anyone reading this book to know God. My relationship with God was the anchor of my stability during my life's storms, and my desire is for people to get to know God for who He is. I think religion has done a disservice to humanity in that people don't have an accurate image of God. Some people aren't interested in having anything to do with God based on how religion painted God to them, even though they respect their fathers' religion as a tradition.

By God's grace, I've been privileged to know God on a personal level. From my personal experience, God has a heart for every individual in the world and is not interested in a specific human-made religious group. God is always after our hearts, and He is eager to have a personal relationship with each of us. "For God so loved the world, that he gave his only begotten Son, that whosoever believeth in him should not perish, but have everlasting life" (John 3:16 KJV).

God has richly given you all things to enjoy. 2 Peter 1:3 (KJV) says, "According as his divine power hath given unto us all things that pertain unto life and godliness, through the knowledge of him that hath called us to glory and virtue." Enjoy your life to the fullest; everything you require to that effect has been given to you. Remember, God gave you His life. Therefore, your faith should be anchored on what Christ came to do, what He's accomplished for you and in you.

Christ already made divine health, divine comfort, divine consolation, a life of endless victories and blessings available to us. Our focus and trust should be on Him, what He's done and who He is, not on our works. Now, because of what Jesus did, we're holy and without blame before the Father. We can boldly stand in the presence of God without guilt, inferiority, or condemnation. We don't have to feel insecure or uncertain about our place with God. Be bold, confident, assured, and glad you belong to Him; He brought you into oneness with Himself. Hallelujah. No matter where you've been, what you've done, how deep in sin you think you've been, you don't have to run away from God. He said in Isaiah 1:18 (KJV), ". . . though your sins be as scarlet, they shall be as white as snow; though they be red like crimson, they shall be as wool." Embrace His love.

Jesus came and fulfilled the plan of God. He was crucified in our place. He paid the full price for man's sin, and then God raised Him to give us the inheritance. Colossians 1:12 (KJV) says, "Giving thanks unto the Father, which hath made us meet to be partakers of the inheritance of the saints in light." Now that God has given us the inheritance through Jesus Christ, there's no reason to hope for it. "Hope" (Jesus) came and completely fulfilled everything God sent Him to give and do for us. Hallelujah! Everything you could ever desire of God has been consummated, accomplished, and granted to you in Jesus Christ. You now must act your faith. Trust Him with your life. Perhaps you've never realized this before; this is your moment.

MAKE JESUS THE LORD OF YOUR LIFE

Avoiding God doesn't make life any easier or better. In fact, no matter how rich or poor we are, the moment we start our connection to God and acknowledge Him in our life, our purpose in life starts to have a meaning. There's a void in humanity that no one can fill except the Creator, and it's never satisfied until we make that connection with Him. I trust that you've been blessed by this book, and it provided you some insight. Now, let me personally invite you to the most important decision of your life—to make Jesus Christ the Lord of your life and connect to God by praying and believing in the following prayer of salvation:

O Lord God, I come to You in the Name of Jesus Christ. Your Word says, *"...whosoever shall call on the name of the Lord shall be saved"* (Acts 2:21, NIV). I ask Jesus to come into my heart to be the Lord of my life, and I receive eternal life into my spirit. According to Romans 10.9-10 (NIV), "If you declare with your mouth, "Jesus is Lord," and believe in your heart that God raised him from the dead, you will be saved. For it is with your heart that you believe and are justified, and it is with your mouth that you profess your faith and are saved." I declare that I am saved; I am born-again; I am a child of God! I now have Christ dwelling in me, and greater is He that is in me than he that is in the world! (1 John 4:4, NIV) I now walk in the consciousness of my new life in Christ Jesus. Hallelujah! Amen!

MY PRAYER FOR YOU

Dear Father,

I thank you for the privilege of prayer. I pray for the people who want to be saved all around the world that they are strengthened with might by your Spirit in their inner man. I pray that the eyes of their heart may be enlightened in order that they may know the hope to which You have called them. Please reveal to them the riches of Your glorious inheritance in Your holy people. I declare that God's word of righteousness, salvation, healing, prosperity, deliverance, comfort, and blessings is producing results in them, forming in them the character and mind of Christ, in Jesus' Name.

Amen.

APPENDIX I

DISCUSSION POINTS/THOUGHTS

Whether you are grieving alone or have a group of people supporting you, I believe the following discussion points will help you assess your situation and provide you ten practical guidance. Please feel free to take what works for you and discard the rest. (All of the following Bible verses are taken from the New International Version.)

1. Lean on God and check your attitude

"Each heart knows its own bitterness, and no one else can share its joy" (Proverbs 4:10).

• Everyone grieves and heals differently. Identify what helps you most. Write them down and share them with your group.

- Some people find relief by talking to others, and some people prefer to process things quietly. Generally, it's advisable to share your thoughts and feelings with your close friends or a therapist.

- Some people get relief by crying. However, it doesn't mean because someone isn't crying, they're strong and are handling it well.

2. Is it better to grieve by myself, or do I need to accept help from others?

"Two are better than one, because they have a good return for their labor: If either of them falls down, one can help the other up. But pity anyone who falls and has no one to help them up" (Ecclesiastes 4:9-10).

- You don't always have to hang out with others; however, don't push away the people who sincerely would like to help you.

- Allocate some time to be alone and to be with others.

- The support from friends and family is critical; please don"t take it for granted.

3. How is my self-care? Am I exercising and eating healthy?

"After all, no one ever hated their own body, but they feed and care for their body, just as Christ does the church" (Ephesians 5:29).

- Eating a balanced diet helps our bodies overcome the stress of grieving. Try to eat fruits and vegetables.

- Drink lots of water.

- If you lost your appetite, try to eat a small portion frequently. You can also consult with your doctor if there would be any beneficial supplements that you can consider.

- Exercise, such as a fast walk or jogging, can help reduce stress.

4. Get enough sleep

"Better one handful with tranquility than two handfuls with toil and chasing after the wind" (Ecclesiastes 4:6).

- Grieving drains your energy; making sure you get sufficient rest is essential.

- Avoid consuming caffeine because it may disrupt your sleep.

- Do light exercise and listen to soft, soothing songs before bed to help distract your mind from the grief.

5. Avoid things that would entangle you with a bad consequence

". . . dear friends, let us purify ourselves from everything that contaminates body and spirit, perfecting holiness out of reverence for God." (2 Corinthians 7:1).

- Some grieving people depend on alcohol and drugs to numb their pain. The relief gained that way is not only temporary, but it could also get you into a harmful trap.

- In some cultures, I have witnessed the women physically hurt themselves that led to long-term physical and emotional damage.

6. Take a break and relax

"There is a time for everything, and a season for every activity under the heavens: 4a time to weep and a time to laugh, a time to mourn and a time to dance." (Ecclesiastes 3:1,4).

- Don't feel guilty about taking time to relax and doing activities you enjoy.

- Spend some time with your friends.

- Try new things.

- Instead of always thinking about your loss, try intentionally focusing on things that will help you move forward.

7. Don't make big decisions in haste

"The plans of the diligent lead to profit as surely as haste leads to poverty." (Proverbs 21:5).

- If possible, take some time before you make any decision that would impact your life.

- Ask for an extension from the authorities if you have to take care of any legal matters.

- Spend some time in prayer before you make any changes.

8. Cherish the memory of the loved one

"Remember the days of old..." (Deuteronomy 32:7).

• Most grieving people like to save things that would help them cherish the loved one's memory, such as handwritten letters, pictures, and personal items.

• Document and save some items that help you cherish the memory of your loved one.

9. Help others

"The Lord Jesus himself said: 'It is more blessed to give than to receive'" (Acts 20:35).

• When you help others, it'll help you reduce the stress of grieving.

• Pray and comfort others who are grieving; by doing so, you will get some comfort.

• Helping and comforting others also gives you self-satisfaction.

10. Check your priorities

"It is better to go to a house of mourning than to go to a house of feasting, for death is the destiny of everyone; the living should take this to heart" (Ecclesiastes 7:2).

• Grieving can help you understand what's essential in life.

• What are you doing with the life you have?

• Always check your priorities and make necessary adjustments.

APPENDIX II

MEDITATION VERSES

The most important key that our beloved Pastor Leon Fontain implanted in my heart is to pray the word of God and declare the promises of God in my life. The following scriptures address the gravity of different types of loss while reminding us of the great strength we can draw from our faith. Please read them loud and meditate on them (All of the scriptures are taken from the New International Version):

- *Matthew 5:1-3*
  Now when Jesus saw the crowds, he went up on a mountainside and sat down. His disciples came to him, and he began to teach them. He said: "Blessed are the poor in spirit, for theirs is the kingdom of heaven."

- *Psalm 73:26*
  My flesh and my heart may fail, but God is the strength of my heart and my portion forever.

- *John 11:25-26*
  Jesus said to her, "I am the resurrection and the life. The one who believes in me will live, even though they die; and whoever lives by believing in me will never die. Do you believe this?"

- *1 Corinthians 15:42-44*
  So will it be with the resurrection of the dead. The body that is sown is perishable, it is raised imperishable; it is sown in dishonor, it is raised in glory; it is sown in weakness, it is raised in power; and it is sown a natural body, it is raised a spiritual body. If there is a natural body, there is also a spiritual body.

- *2 Corinthians 4:17-18*
  For our light and momentary troubles are achieving for us an eternal glory that far outweighs them all. So we fix our eyes not on what is seen, but on what is unseen, since what is seen is temporary, but what is unseen is eternal.

- *2 Corinthians 5:8*
  We are confident, I say, and would prefer to be away from the body and at home with the Lord.

- *Romans 14:8*
  If we live, we live for the Lord; and if we die, we die for the Lord. So, whether we live or die, we belong to the Lord.

- Revelation 21:4
  "He will wipe every tear from their eyes. There will be no more death' or mourning or crying or pain, for the old order of things has passed away."

- Psalm 34:18
  The LORD is close to the brokenhearted and saves those who are crushed in spirit.

- Psalm 147:3
  He heals the brokenhearted and binds up their wounds.

- John 14:1
  "Do not let your hearts be troubled. You believe in God; believe also in me."

- Joshua 1:9
  "Have I not commanded you? Be strong and courageous. Do not be afraid; do not be discouraged, for the LORD your God will be with you wherever you go."

- Romans 8:28
  And we know that in all things God works for the good of those who love him, who have been called according to his purpose.

- Matthew 5:4
  Blessed are those who mourn, for they will be comforted.

- 1 Thessalonians 4:13-14
  Brothers and sisters, we do not want you to be uninformed about those who sleep in death, so that you do not grieve like the rest of mankind, who have no hope. For we believe that Jesus died and rose again, and so we

*believe that God will bring with Jesus those who have
fallen asleep in him.*

- *1 Thessalonians 4:17-18*
  *After that, we who are still alive and are left will be
  caught up together with them in the clouds to meet the
  Lord in the air. And so we will be with the Lord forever.
  Therefore encourage one another with these words.*

- *Philippians 2:20*
  *I have no one else like him, who will show genuine
  concern for your welfare.*

- *Matthew 19:14*
  *But Jesus said, "Let the little children come to me and
  do not hinder them, for to such belongs the kingdom of
  heaven."*

- *Matthew 18:14*
  *So it is not the will of my Father who is in heaven that
  one of these little ones should perish.*

- *John 14:27*
  *Peace I leave with you; my peace I give to you. Not as
  the world gives do I give to you. Let not your hearts be
  troubled, neither let them be afraid.*

- *Luke 18:15-17*
  *Now they were bringing even infants to him that he
  might touch them. And when the disciples saw it, they
  rebuked them. But Jesus called them to him, saying,
  "Let the children come to me, and do not hinder them,
  for to such belongs the kingdom of God. Truly, I say to
  you, whoever does not receive the kingdom of God like a
  child shall not enter it."*

- *Psalm 48:14*
  For this God is our God for ever and ever; he will be
  our guide even to the end.

- *Isaiah 57:1-2*
  The righteous perish, and no one takes it to heart; the
  devout are taken away, and no one understands that the
  righteous are taken away to be spared from evil. Those
  who walk uprightly enter into peace; they find rest as
  they lie in death.

- *Isaiah 41:10*
  Fear not, for I am with you; be not dismayed, for I am
  your God; I will strengthen you, I will help you, I will
  uphold you with my righteous right hand.

- *2 Corinthians 1:3-4*
  who comforts us in all our affliction so that we will be
  able to comfort those who are in any affliction with the
  comfort with which we ourselves are comforted by God.

- *Genesis 24:67*
  Then Isaac brought her into his mother Sarah's tent, and
  he took Rebekah, and she became his wife, and he loved
  her; thus, Isaac was comforted after his mother's death.

- *Lamentations 3:31-32*
  For the Lord will not reject forever, For if He causes
  grief, Then He will have compassion According to His
  abundant lovingkindness.

- *John 16:22*
  "Therefore you too have grief now; but I will see you
  again, and your heart will rejoice, and no one will take
  your joy away from you."

- *Psalm 9:9*
  The LORD also will be a stronghold for the oppressed, A stronghold in times of trouble.

- *Psalm 46:1*
  God is our refuge and strength, an ever-present help in trouble.

- *Isaiah 57:1-2*
  The righteous man perishes, and no one lays it to heart; devout men are taken away, while no one understands. For the righteous man is taken away from calamity; he enters into peace; they rest in their beds who walk in their uprightness.

- *1 Corinthians 15:55*
  "O death, where is your victory? O death, where is your sting?"

- *Revelation 14:13*
  Then I heard a voice from heaven say, "Write this: Blessed are the dead who die in the Lord from now on." "Yes," says the Spirit, "they will rest from their labor, for their deeds will follow them."

- *John 14:1-2*
  "Do not let your hearts be troubled. You believe in God; believe also in me. My Father's house has many rooms; if that were not so, would I have told you that I am going there to prepare a place for you?"

- *1 John 3:2*
  Dear friends, now we are children of God, and what we will be has not yet been made known. But we know that

when Christ appears, we shall be like him, for we shall see him as he is.

- *Romans 8:18*
  For I consider that the sufferings of this present time are not worth comparing with the glory that is to be revealed to us.

- *Luke 20:36*
  For they cannot die anymore, because they are equal to angels and are sons of God, being sons of the resurrection.

APPENDIX III
WORKS CITED

1. Angelou, Maya **When I Think of Death,** "Popular Reading" http://www.funeral-helper.org/popular-reading-when-i-think-of-death-maya-angelou-.html , Accessed September 12, 2020

2. Bass, David N. "Griefshare." https://www.griefshare.org/about.

3. "Chen (Hebrew Term 2580)." *Old Testament Hebrew Lexical Dictionary – New American Standard,* Blue Letter Bible Institute. https://www.blueletterbible.org/

4. "Divine Grace." *Wikipedia, Wikimedia Foundation,* 6 January 2021, https://en.wikipedia.org/wiki/

Divine_grace#:~:text=Divine%20grace%20is%20 a%20theological,or%20excellence%20of%20 divine%20origin.

5. "Divine Grace" and "Charis χάρις." Strong, James (2001), *The Strongest Strong's Exhaustive Concordance of the Bible*, Zondervan.

6. "Grace." *Merriam-Webster.com Dictionary*, Miriam-Webster, https://www.merriam-webster.com/ dictionary/grace. Accessed Jan 12, 2021.

7. BibleGateway App. HarperCollins Christian Publishing, 2020. Vers. 3.14. Apple App Store/ Google Play Store, https://apps.apple.com/app/apple-store/ id506512797

8. Davis, Tchiki. "Self-Care: 12 ways to take better care of yourself," *Psychology Today*, https://www.psychol-ogytoday.com/ca/blog/click-here-happiness/201812/ self-care-12-ways-take-better-care-yourself.

9. Duffin, Erin. "Deaths in Canada 2020." October 5, 2020, *Statista*.

10. Fontaine, Leon "Devoted." https://miraclechannel. ca/devoted//.

11. Fontaine, Leon. "Why does God allow?" *YouTube*, Intro music by Joel Houston and Ben Fielding and Brooke Ligerwood, May 14, 2020, https://www.you-tube.com/watch?v=RHKRfBgjVEI&t=2446s.

12. Hairston, Stephanie. "Grief," *TheRecoveryVillage. com*, The Recovery Village Umatilla Drug and Alcohol Rehab, https://www.therecoveryvillage.com/ mental-health/grief/.

13. HQLines.Tumblr.com. "When Life Gives You Every Reason to be Negative..." *Pinterest,* https://www.pinterest.ca/pin/560135889092147523/.

14. Oyakhilome, Chris. "Training yourself In The Faith-Life," *FLATimes.* Christ Embassy International, https://flatimes.com/rhapsody-realities-22-may-2020-training-faith-life/.

15. Pogue, David. "What to say (and what not to say) to someone who's grieving." *The New York Times,* Feb. 14,2019, https://www.nytimes.com/2019/02/14/smarter-living/what-to-say-and-what-not-to-say-to-someone-whos-grieving.html.

16. Scott, Chet. "BUILT TO LEAD – Together We Transform" Accessed: October 29, 2019.

17. Sikha, Aruna "The stages that a Grieving Person Goes Through." *Online Counselling Blogs,* May 28, 2019, https://www.mywellnesshub.in/blog/the-stages-that-a-grieving-person-goes-through.

18. Statistics Canada *"Deaths, 2018"* The Daily - https://www150.statcan.gc.ca/n1/daily-quotidien/191126/dq191126c-eng.htm, Published November 26, 2019, Accessed Feb 2, 2021

19. TerKeurst, Lysa. "What Jesus Longs for Us to Know Today." *Proverbs31.org,* Proverbs 31 Ministries, Feb. 22, 2018, https://proverbs31.org/read/devotions/full-post/2018/02/22/what-jesus-longs-for-us-to-know-today.

20. *The Bible.* Amplified Bible (AMP), Zondervan and The Lockman Foundation, 2015.

21. *The Bible.* Amplified Bible Classic Version (AMPC), The Lockman Foundation, 1987.

22. *The Bible*. Good News Translation (GNT), American Bible Society, 1976.

23. *The Bible*. King James Version (KJV).

24. *The Bible*. New International Version (NIV), Zondervan, 1978.

25. *The Bible*. New King James Version (NKJV), James Nelson, 1982.

26. *The Bible*. New Living Translation (NLT), Tyndale House Foundation, 2007.

27. Ward, Stanley. "Spiritual Gifts: Listed by Paul, Motivated by Love." *CrossWalk*, Salem Web Network, https://www.crosswalk.com/faith/spiritual-life/ spiritual-gifts-listed-by-paul-mmotivated-by-love. html.

28. Webster, Bill. "10 Facts about Grief and Grieving." *Sturm Funeral & Cremation Services*, https://sturmfh. com/9/10-Facts-about-Grief-and-Grieving.html. Accessed August 8, 2020.

29. Webster, Bill. "Grief journey." Griefjourney.com.

30. World Health Organization "*Coronavirus disease (COVID-19)*," https://www.who.int/emergencies/ diseases/novel-coronavirus-2019. Accessed February 2, 2021.

31. Xu, Jiaquan, et al. "Mortality in the United States." January 2020. https://www.cdc.gov/nchs/products/ databriefs/db355.htm#Summary.

ACKNOWLEDGEMENTS

To God, who bestowed upon me immeasurable grace throughout my life, Aba Father, my confidence is in You, and I am 100% dependent on Your grace. Thank you! To my late husband, Isaiah, you were able to deliver love to everyone who had the privilege to know you, despite your struggles. I have been blessed to have you in my life. You have taught me how to love unconditionally. To my beloved firstborn, Joseph, you have been stretching my personal growth to match your talents. You are thoughtful, compassionate, and have been very supportive throughout my journey. I thank God who blessed you with wisdom beyond your age, and I continue to declare blessings in your coming in and blessings in your going out; you are a true blessing from God to me. My beloved daughter, Faith, you have been stretching my patience through your imagination, creativity, and leadership. I enjoy your artistic, unstructured, yet beautiful world of a little girl. You are more than I can ever dream of; I declare expansion of creativity upon your life, and may God make you a solution to a troubled world and enlarge your territory. Remain blessed, my sweet darling. My delightful Eliora, I'm honoured to have you in my life. You have been a source of joy and comfort to me. You have always exceeded my imagination, and I can't wait to see what you can achieve in life. I have enjoyed your company throughout this journey, and you are an angel, a messenger of God to your world. What a fantastic blessing to have a hugely gifted daughter! So grateful to God for His blessing. My beloved son and daughters may God continue to bless you and enlarge your territory.

To my siblings Elsa Araya, Yordanos Araya, Mullugeta Araya, Amanuel Araya, Temesgen Araya, Semhar Araya, and their families, who have always been there whenever I needed you. Particularly Semhar, I will never forget your dedication to support me throughout the tough years. You have made me able to attend different seminars, grief share sessions, and women's retreats without worries about my kids. What can I say? May God bless you beyond your expectations and imagination. To my dearest brothers Biniam Keleta and Gebremical Fishatsion, who have been my emergency line throughout the years. I can call you for anything anytime, and you'd be on it before we finish our conversation. To my beloved brothers Kidane Hagos and Dawit Hagos - you are my cheerleaders. Thank you for believing in me. I am truly blessed by your ongoing encouragement and support.

To Isaiah's siblings: Zewdi Tekle, Fishaye Tekle, Mihret Tekle, Belaynesh Tekle, Sirak Tekle, and their families; to my beloved spiritual mentors and Pastors, Chris Oyakhilome, Daniel Mehari (Danay), Leon Fontaine, Meron Woldehawariat, Naod Gebremeskel, and Olatubosun Sowunmi; to all my beloved GFMM Calgary family; to all Ethiopian and Eritrean churches in Calgary, to ECCAC, and to RCCG House of David Calgary; to Yeshi Mohammed's family and Thomas Belayneh's family; to Dale Wolaniuk, Monique Ferguson, and my Celero

Solutions Inc. family, to my God-given friends, sisters, and brothers throughout the planet, especially to Asmara University and Ås Life Science University alumni; Thank you for your great support during my bereavement.

To my friends and neighbours from New Brighton: Wondesh, Hirut, Simret, Dani, Lina, Serkie, John, Jenn, Andre, and Melanie, who stood with me in the darkest moment of my life—you have been my support line throughout this journey. To my beloved friends Genet Beyene, Judi Lawrence, Kedija Kedir, Meron Mulugeta, Tsigereda Haile, Awet Tsegay, Martha Ermias, Selam Girmay, Freawet Mega, Temesgen Debessay, Tsehaye Araya, and Saba Mesfin, I cherish our meaningful friendship a lot. To Ashenafi Minasse, Aaron Froese, Dr. Girma Lulu, Aida Maru, Donna Schaffer, Dallas Froese, Deborah Fissha, Lidiah Fissha, Rahel Manaye, Chuchu Alemayehu, Genet Alemayehu, Abayneh Reta, Bethel Abraham, Bereket Alazar, Meron Zewdu, Samuel Getachew, Melake Gebrehiwet, Maasho Solomon, Zewdi Asfaha, Belaynesh Till, Bini Assress's and Daniel Habte's family – thank you for your ongoing prayers and support.

To my dearest friends Dawit Tesfamicael, Roti Akinsanmi, and Dr. Michael Habteyonas for your ongoing support and care; plus, your feedback on my writing were invaluable. To my editor Jill Ellis, for your incredible patience and excellence. To my mentor Dr. Gebru Woldu for believing in me and encouraging me to write this book, and taking the time to review it thoroughly. To Mussie Haddish, my ally, and his beautiful wife Bisrat, I can't find enough words to express my appreciation for your wisdom and support; you have completed every task assigned to you with excellence. To Igniting Souls Tribe and Author Academy Elite, this book won't exist without you. To Pastor Leon and Sally Fontaine and the Springs Church family, for accepting my kids and me into your family the way we are and giving us the environment to heal and thrive. Great appreciation to everyone who has been thinking, supporting and praying for my family; this book is the fruit of your support, encouragement and prayers. May God bless you all!

ABOUT THE AUTHOR

Simret Araya Ghebremariam was born and raised in Asmara, Eritrea (a small country in East Africa). Soon after completing her bachelor's degree at Asmara University, she was awarded a scholarship from the University of Life Science, Norway, to complete her master's degree in Natural Resources Management and Sustainable Development. After completing her education in Norway, her country's political condition made it impossible for her to go back to her homeland. She moved to Canada in 2002 where she shifted her profession from Environmental Science to IT project management.

Simret's passion is always on helping people to feel better and get better. Her integrity and authentic leadership style earned her great respect from clients, friends and colleagues. She's a senior consultant and runs a couple of businesses, including coaching leaders to achieve their best by cultivating the best version within them. She's a certified life coach and a tribe member of Igniting Souls. She is one of the leaders and mentors serving the Eritrean and Ethiopian communities in Calgary, and she has been supporting orphans in different refugee camps in Ethiopia. Recently, the Eritrean school board members elected Simret to be the principal of the Eritrean Heritage and Cultural School in Calgary.

Simret is a mother of three vibrant children, and she has been inspiring many people through her blogs and poems on her social media and websites. She has also connected several volunteers with homeless people and promoting mental health awareness under her "Isaiah Cares" charity program to continue her husband's legacy, who, in life, was striving to make Calgary a better place.

HOW CAN I CONTACT THE AUTHOR?

Simret is a certified life coach, who helps people and organizations to discover and maximize their potential. If you feel stuck in any situation, she would love to help you move forward. If you would like to start a journey from despair to strength, to live a life of meaning and purpose, visit her website at www.unhackabledestiny.ca.

CPSIA information can be obtained
at www.ICGtesting.com
Printed in the USA
BVHW031500280421
606034BV00003B/51/J